STAAR

SUCCESS STRATEGIES

Grade 7
Reading

STAAR Test Review for the
State of Texas Assessments of Academic Readiness

Dear Future Exam Success Story:

Congratulations on your purchase of our study guide. Our goal in writing our study guide was to cover the content on the test, as well as provide insight into typical test taking mistakes and how to overcome them.

Standardized tests are a key component of being successful, which only increases the importance of doing well in the high-pressure high-stakes environment of test day. How well you do on this test will have a significant impact on your future- and we have the research and practical advice to help you execute on test day.

The product you're reading now is designed to exploit weaknesses in the test itself, and help you avoid the most common errors test takers frequently make.

How to use this study guide

We don't want to waste your time. Our study guide is fast-paced and fluff-free. We suggest going through it a number of times, as repetition is an important part of learning new information and concepts.

First, read through the study guide completely to get a feel for the content and organization. Read the general success strategies first, and then proceed to the content sections. Each tip has been carefully selected for its effectiveness.

Second, read through the study guide again, and take notes in the margins and highlight those sections where you may have a particular weakness.

Finally, bring the manual with you on test day and study it before the exam begins.

Your success is our success

We would be delighted to hear about your success. Send us an email and tell us your story. Thanks for your business and we wish you continued success-

Sincerely,

Mometrix Test Preparation Team

Need more help? Check out our flashcards at: http://MometrixFlashcards.com/STAAR

TABLE OF CONTENTS

Top 15 Test Taking Tips

1. Know the test directions, duration, topics, question types, how many questions
2. Setup a flexible study schedule at least 3-4 weeks before test day
3. Study during the time of day you are most alert, relaxed, and stress free
4. Maximize your learning style; visual learner use visual study aids, auditory learner use auditory study aids
5. Focus on your weakest knowledge base
6. Find a study partner to review with and help clarify questions
7. Practice, practice, practice
8. Get a good night's sleep; don't try to cram the night before the test
9. Eat a well balanced meal
10. Wear comfortable, loose fitting, layered clothing; prepare for it to be either cold or hot during the test
11. Eliminate the obviously wrong answer choices, then guess the first remaining choice
12. Pace yourself; don't rush, but keep working and move on if you get stuck
13. Maintain a positive attitude even if the test is going poorly
14. Keep your first answer unless you are positive it is wrong
15. Check your work, don't make a careless mistake

Reading Assessment

Structural analysis

The term *structural analysis* refers to looking at the parts of a word and breaking it down into its different components to determine the word's meaning. Parts of a word include prefixes, suffixes, and the root word. A reader can also look at the context of a word, or the words surrounding an unknown word, to figure out meaning. By looking at the root of an unfamiliar word, the reader can get a basic sense of what the word means. For example, the word *joy* means "great happiness" and the suffix *-ful* means "full of". If the reader did not know what the word *joyful* meant, he or she could break the word down into these components to figure out its meaning. The word *joyful*, when looked at in pieces, means "full of happiness". By knowing a multitude of meanings for root words, prefixes, and suffixes, a reader can better understand difficult passages of text.

<u>Example</u>
Use structural analysis to figure out the meaning of the word *mournful* in the following sentence:

> "Well, it being away in the night and stormy, and all so mysterious-like, I felt just the way any other boy would a felt when I see that wreck laying there so *mournful* and lonesome in the middle of the river." (From *The Adventures of Huckleberry Finn* by Mark Twain).

Structural analysis involves breaking a word up into a root word and any prefixes or suffixes to determine the meaning of the complete word. *Mourn* means to grieve for something, while *-ful* refers to being "full of". Putting the two components together, *mournful* means "full of grief or sadness". This definition makes sense in the context of the sentence. The "wreck" in the sentence is sad looking because it is in the river by itself.

When conducting structural analysis, always look for a root word and any prefixes or suffixes that have been added on to the root word. If a component of a word is not familiar, decipher what is clear about the word, then look at the word as used in context.

Prefix and suffix

The term *prefix* refers to an affix that is placed before a root word, or the main part of a word that may come from Latin or Greek origins. A *suffix* refers to an affix that is placed after a root word. *Affix* means to add onto a root word to form a new one. Examples of prefixes include *pre-, dis-, un-, im-, ex-,* or *in-*; suffixes include *-ed, -able,* or *-ful,* among others. The prefix *pre-* means "before"; *dis-, un-, im-,* and *in-* mean "not" and *ex-* means "more". The suffix *-ed* puts a word in the past tense, while the suffix *-able* makes a word into an adjective meaning "capable of". The suffix *-ful* refers to being "full of" and also makes a word into an adjective.

Experience to determine word meaning

The more words a person is exposed to, the greater their vocabulary will become. By reading on a regular basis, a person can increase the number of ways they have seen a word in context. Based on experience, a person can recall how a word was used in the past and apply that knowledge to a new context. For example, a person may have seen the word *gull* used to mean a bird that is found near the seashore. However, a *gull* can also be a person who is easily tricked. If the word is used in context in reference to a character, the reader can recognize that the character is being called a bird that is not seen as extremely intelligent. Using what the reader knows about a word can be useful when making comparisons or figuring out the meaning of a new use of a word, as in figurative language, idioms, analogies, and multiple-meaning words.

Example
Using experience, determine the definition of the multiple-meaning word *basin* in the following sentence:

> The *basin* had filled with water over the summer months, so that the rocky
> bottom was no longer visible to the casual hiker.

A *basin* can be either a bowl filled with water or a depression in the earth. Looking at the context of the word in the sentence, the latter definition is correct in this case. Knowing multiple definitions of a word can help when figuring out which definition applies in a sentence. If the definition of a word is not known, however, look at the context of the word. In the example, the reader knows that the *basin* had to be deep enough to fill with water. The reader also knows that the bottom of the *basin* had been filled with rock, and that the location is outdoors. Hikers are normally able to see the bottom of the *basin*, so it must be a large depression in the earth.

Context Clues

The term context clues refers to words or phrases found in sentences surrounding an unknown word. Context clues may include examples of the unknown word, synonyms, antonyms, definitions, or contrasting information. By using context clues in the surrounding sentences, the reader can figure out approximately what the word means. A context clue indicating an example may contain the unknown word(s) including the phrase 'such as,' a dash, or a colon before stated information. A synonym is a word with a similar meaning to the unknown word, whereas an antonym is a word with the opposite meaning. A definition will state exactly what the unknown word means. Contrasting information will include facts that are different from the unknown word.

Dictionary, Glossary, and Thesaurus

One tool that can be used to build word meanings is the dictionary. A dictionary contains words listed alphabetically. It tells each word's meaning. It also tells the word's part of speech. Dictionaries can be books or be online. Glossaries are like dictionaries, but they are smaller than dictionaries. Glossaries list words alphabetically. They tell each word's meaning. They are found at the back of books, and they list words in the books. A thesaurus is a tool that has synonyms of words. For example, if you look up the word happy in a thesaurus, you would see the words content, pleased, glad, joyful, and delighted. A thesaurus does not give a definition like a dictionary does, but you can use a thesaurus to help figure out the meaning of an unfamiliar word. If you are familiar with some of the synonyms of the word, you can determine a precise meaning of the unfamiliar word. For example, if you looked up the word exultant and saw the synonyms overjoyed and thrilled, this could lead you to its meaning "extremely happy."

Denotative and connotative meaning

The denotative meaning of a word is the literal meaning of a word according to the dictionary. The connotative meaning of a word is a secondary meaning that is implied in the text. A good way to remember the difference between denotative and connotative is to think "direct" or "dictionary" in relation to denotative.

An example of a denotative meaning for the adjective *ablaze* would be "burning", as in the logs burning in a fireplace. A connotative meaning for the adjective *ablaze*, based on the context of the word, may indicate a level of comfort while sitting in front of a fireplace. For instance, in the context: "A logs were *ablaze* in the fireplace, radiating heat out into the corners of the snow-enclosed room", the word *ablaze* implies comfort and coziness within the space described. The connotative meaning of a word can often have an emotional association for the reader.

<u>Example</u>
Define the denotative and connotative meaning of the word *palace* in the following sentence:

> The golden *palace* gates opened slowly to reveal an expansive garden that was well-tended by precise gardeners all wearing the king's insignia.

In the example, the denotative meaning of the word is that a *palace* is literally a place where royalty lives. A *palace* implies, or connotes, a place of riches and is usually associated with wealth. The words "golden", "expansive garden", and "king's insignia" all give clues that the *palace* can be viewed as a place of importance, one that is well taken care of.

When looking for the denotative meaning of a word, remember to think "direct", or the literal meaning of the word. The connotative meaning of the word is implied and not directly stated; the connotative meaning is often associated with emotion and feeling about the typical context of the word.

Derivative of a word

The derivative of a word is the final product after a word has undergone a change from its original form. For example, the word *fruit* refers to seed-containing products of a tree or plant that are often consumed by humans. If a prefix or suffix is added onto the root word *fruit*, the meaning of the word is changed. The suffix *-ful* added onto *fruit* to form the word *fruitful* would mean "full of fruit" or, more accurately, "abundant growth". Note that the meaning of the derivative, or final word form, changed from the meaning of the root word. If a word has been changed from its original form, it can have an entirely different meaning based on what prefixes or suffixes have been added onto the root word.

Autobiography

An autobiography is a story that an author writes about himself. Autobiographies normally encompass the majority of the person's life. Many start with a description of childhood and go well into adult life. The author normally tries to stay as factual as possible, but may include a great deal of commentary as well. A diary is an informal type of autobiography. It tells not only the author's story, but also includes much detail about thoughts and emotions along the way.

An autobiography can also be written as a fictional narrative. Many times an author will write his story, but use different names and modify details to maintain anonymity. The author may not be proud of his past actions, and writing about his life without admitting that the story is true is one way he can discuss his past without incriminating himself. An author might also write a story where he explores what might have happened in his life if past situations had been different.

Theme

The *theme* of a story is a unifying idea that is used throughout the text; it can take the form of a common setting, idea, symbol, design, or recurring event. For example, a series of events in a story may be based upon people being willing to trust the actions of others. The story may be centered on why people need to trust others in order to carry out important actions. For example, a character may trust that a bus driver will stay on the road while the bus driver, in turn, trusts that the passengers stay in their seats so that they do not distract him. The *theme* of a story may vary according to place, time, and characters, but *theme* is often based on common human experience. A plot line is built around the theme of a story.

Purpose of text

The purpose of a text is the author's main reason for writing the story. When the author decides to change the purpose of the text, the entire story is changed. For example, an author may write a story to inform the reader about a given topic, such as the need to stay hydrated during hot weather. If the author decides to change the purpose of the text to persuade the reader to drink a particular type of sports beverage to stay hydrated during hot weather, the text becomes an advertisement. While the original purpose of the text was to inform, the new purpose of the text is to persuade. Changing the purpose of a text can alter the length of the story, the type of words used (descriptive vs. sensational), and the amount of information included. An author will often use positive expert testimonials when trying to persuade the reader to accept a given point-of-view, while the author will simply include sources of information for an informative piece.

Example 1
Read the following sentence from *The Tale of Benny Badger*. State the author's point in writing the sentence, whether it is to inform, entertain, persuade, or state an opinion.
>   He had a powerful body, short, stout legs, and big feet, which bore long,
>   strong claws.

The author wishes to inform the reader about the character in his story. The example sentence includes a description of the character's physical attributes; describing the character so that the reader can picture what they look like in the scene. The entire story may be meant to entertain the reader, but the sentence is providing factual information about a character. By informing the reader about the character's attributes, the author is giving the reader background information on why the character may act a certain way in an event further along in the story.

The author is not persuading the reader to accept a point of view, the information presented is not an opinion on an issue, and the author does not have a personal motivation for presenting the information. The text is meant to inform the reader through description.

- 5 -

<u>Example 2</u>
Read the following sentence. State the author's point in writing the sentence, whether it is to inform, entertain, persuade, or state an opinion.

> The cat buried itself deep in the crinkled paper bag, until only a soft black nose and long whiskers could be seen by innocent passersby.

The example sentence is meant to entertain and inform the reader. The author uses description to tell the audience where the cat is located and what it looks like. The sentence is merely for entertainment, not meant as a presentation of important information. In the example, the reader can picture the cat crouched in a bag, ready to pounce on something that walks by. By using description to paint a picture of the scene in the reader's mind, the author is forming the background for events that occur in the story.

When an author wishes to persuade the audience about a given topic, they will take a single point of view on an issue. If an author is stating their opinion, the sentence will be based on what the author believes to have occurred, not what is actually visible to each passerby.

Conventions in mythology

Some of the more common conventions in mythology are the extended simile, the hero's task, the quest, and the circle story. In an extended simile, the author introduces a simile and gives extraordinary detail about the object that is being used as the simile. Often, the extended simile will be used to provide a pause or rest in the story. The extended simile is also referred to as the Homeric simile or the epic simile. The hero's task refers to the task or tasks that the hero must accomplish over the course of the story. These will often include feats that seem impossible at first glance. The quest is a common type of hero's task. It usually involves the hero traveling a great distance and overcoming many obstacles to obtain something or someone and then return home. Broadly speaking, a circle story is a story that comes full circle in the end. Some situation is put off-balance at the beginning and by the end, it has been righted. For example, if the hero is forced to leave his home at the beginning of the story, he returns home in the end.

Setting

The setting is where a story takes place. The setting of a story may stay the same for the entire story, or change as events in the story unfold. For example, an entire story may take place in one room or cross continents as the reader follows the characters along on a trail of events.

The setting of a story is described by the author in terms of what it looks like, how the character feels and anything else that is happening at that location at the time. For example, a character may be caught on a doorstep on a cold, rainy day. The character may feel frustrated as they shiver in the doorway, waiting for the heavy rain to let up a bit.

<u>Perception of a story based on setting</u>
The setting of a story can allow the reader to employ preconceived notions about where the story takes place based on their own experience. If a story takes place on a farm, the reader will picture a rural, peaceful setting, which may go along with, or be in contrast to, the actual plot of the story. For example, a reader would not expect a scary story to occur on a farm on a sunny day. A reader may, in contrast, view a dark subway as a dangerous place,

while the plot of a story set there may be based on a very calm series of events. When an author is crafting a story, they need to consider what the audience may already think about a particular setting in order to properly present the events of a story for greatest impact.

Graphical elements in poem

Graphic elements in a poem such as capitalization, line length, and word position can call special attention to words or phrases. Capitalization can signal the beginning of a sentence, or all caps may be used to provide emphasis. Line length can be used to help create a shape, like in concrete poems, or to create a bold statement, like a one word line. Word position can be used to contribute to a feeling or it can also be used to help create a shape.

Dialogue and stage directions

Dialogue is basically what the characters say in a play. This can be through talking to each other, talking to themselves, or even talking to the audience. The type of speech, word choice, and accent a character uses is specific to the role he is playing. For example, a person cast to play a cowboy would have certain words in his vocabulary that a character from a big city in the north would not have.

A playwright also uses stage directions to make the play flow smoothly. Character interaction helps the viewer to understand the mood of the scene. If two characters are confrontational, the viewer is aware that there is some type of conflict occurring. Stage directions create order when all the characters are on stage together.

Creating a plot

All plots begin with a setting, where the story takes place. In some stories the plot is more obvious than in others. Setting plays a key role in the progression of events in some stories and is less intertwined in the plot of other stories. In order for a plot to develop, it must include characters, which can be human or another type of entity. A plot will start at one point, either before a conflict occurs, after a conflict occurs, or in the middle of a conflict. The plot will continue to develop by the introduction of new ideas and events centered on the main conflict in the story. The action in the story will rise until a climax is reached within the conflict. At the climax of a story, a decision is made and the action winds down; this is called the denouement. The conflict is usually resolved in some way by the end of the story. Some conflicts are left open-ended, so that the reader is left to decide what really happened at the end of the story.

Events in plot sequence

Read the following plot and analyze what event is missing from the plot sequence.
> Martin's family decided to go camping at the local park over the weekend.
> They packed all the camping necessities and drove to the park. Thick sheets
> of rain poured down all day, so that they were stuck in their tent.

Martin and his family forgot to check the weather forecast before they left for their camping trip. To fill in the missing detail, the author may write: "Martin and his family checked the forecast and saw that it was going to rain, but decided to go camping anyway." The flow of the story is broken up by the sudden realization that it is raining, something that could be prevented by adding in the missing detail.

When details are missing from a plot sequence, the audience has trouble following the action in a story. By adding in additional details, the point of each step in a story can be made clearer to the audience.

Point of view

An author may use first, second, or third person point of view in a text. First person point of view is written from the perspective of one character. Use of the pronouns 'I', 'me', 'we', and 'my' indicate that the author is using first person point of view. Second person point of view uses the pronoun 'you' when telling the story to another person. Second person point of view is the least commonly used point of view. Third person point of view tells a story from an all-knowing, or omniscient, perspective. The reader can get into the thoughts and points of view of multiple characters in a story when third person point of view is used.

Figurative language

Figurative language is language that goes beyond the literal meaning of the words. Descriptive language that evokes imagery in the reader's mind is one type of figurative language. Exaggeration is also one type of figurative language. Also, when you compare two things, you are using figurative language. Similes and metaphors are ways of comparing things, and both are types of figurative language commonly found in poetry. An example of figurative language (a simile in this case) is: The child howled like a coyote when her mother told her to pick up the toys. In this example, the child's howling is compared to that of a coyote. Figurative language is descriptive in nature and helps the reader understand the sound being made in this sentence.

Style, tone, and mood

Style, *tone*, and *mood* all play an important role in the development of a story. The *style* of a story refers to whether the author uses short, choppy sentences, long, elaborate sentences, formal language, or informal language. The *tone* of a story refers to the attitude conveyed by a story, such as one of anger, happiness, or drama. The *mood* of a story is the overall feeling conveyed by a setting. For example, a story may be dark in terms of setting, characters, and events that occur. The reader's impression of a story can vary based on the *style*, *tone*, and *mood* established by the author. If a story is presented in a picturesque countryside location where the characters are content and the style of speaking is elaborate, the reader will have a different impression of the story than if the setting is in a rundown house with a pale, unhappy caretaker that rarely speaks.

Example 1
Read the following sentences. Describe how the mood of the sentences can be changed by the author.

> The waves crashed loudly against the rough peaks of the shore, sending shivers up Madeleine's spine. Dark clouds rolled in from the open sea, signaling an incoming storm.

The author uses adjectives and adverbs in the sentence to build a mood of worry and dark suspense in the setting. To change the mood of the text, the author can simply change the adjectives and adverbs used to describe the scene. For example, the following revision would make the mood of the sentences more calm and inviting: The waves lapped softly up the rounded dunes of the shore, soothing Madeleine's thoughts. Sun rays shone down from the open sky, signaling a day of calm waters.

The way an author chooses to describe a scene sets the mood of the story. An author will plan how he or she wants the scene to sound to the reader, then use the necessary adjectives and adverbs to describe the scene he or she envisions.

Example 2
Read the following sentences. Describe the style and tone that are used by the author.
    At precisely 8:55 am, he arrived at the heavy front door of the library. He glanced at the gold watch on his left wrist before pausing to tap his polished black shoes with impatience.

The style used by the author in the sentences is matter-of-fact and descriptive. The author uses proper grammar and full sentences, making the tone very formal. The reader gets a sense of urgency from the tone of the sentences, based on the character arriving "precisely" at a certain time, "glancing at his watch", and "tapping his shoes with impatience".

An author can choose the type of words to include in a paragraph based upon the image that he or she wants to portray to the audience. The author builds anticipation by using words in the example that show urgency. The audience is encouraged to read more and find out what happens next by the author's choice of words in the selection.

Explicit vs. implicit information in a text

Explicit information is information that is stated in a text. It is not something that is hinted at. A nonfiction text is usually made up of a main idea and supporting details. These supporting details are explicit: they are stated right in the text. They can be used to support an inference that is not stated in the text, or to support the main claims of an essay. Supporting information should be based on fact, not opinion. It should come from a reliable source and be something that others can verify. When trying to find textual evidence for what a text says explicitly, you will need to look for details that give more information about it.

Implicit information is information that is not directly stated in a text, but can be inferred from something that the author explicitly states. For instance, the author may say "Seth buys a new TV, laptop, and home theater system every year." From this the reader could infer several things. For instance, Seth probably likes electronics and has a lot of spending money.

Media influences

Television is one of many media used to affect a person's emotions, and also behavior. Different images, words, graphics, and sounds can be used to create meaning. For example, advertisements directed at children will often show other kids having fun doing an activity. The bright colors and obvious excitement on their faces will entice a child watching the advertisement to want the item. The child sees other kids having fun, and wants to have fun too. Adults can be influenced by media in much the same way.

Journalists will write positive stories about a person or product that encourages the adult to want to try a product or back a certain person because of the results they read about. Images can also be used to appeal to a person's emotions. A sad image such as a neglected animal or a starving child will often result in compassion from the viewer and can even spur the viewer to some action, such as donating money to a cause.

Making Inferences

An inference is a conclusion or generalization that the reader makes based on the information provided within a text. Certain facts are included to help a reader come to a specific conclusion. For example, a story may open with a man trudging through the snow on a cold winter day, dragging a sled behind him. The reader can logically infer from the setting of the story that the man is wearing heavy winter clothes in order to stay warm. Information is implied based on the setting of a story, which is why setting is an important element of the text. If the same man in the example was trudging down a beach on a hot summer day, dragging a surf board behind him, the reader would assume that the man is not wearing heavy clothes. The reader makes inferences based on their own experiences and the information presented to them in the story.

Text evidence

The term *text evidence* refers to information that supports a main point or points in a story. Information used as *text evidence* is precise, descriptive, and factual. A main point is often followed by supporting details that provide evidence to back-up a claim. For example, a story may include the claim that winter occurs during opposite months in the Northern and Southern hemispheres. *Text evidence* based on this claim may include countries where winter occurs in opposite months, along with reasons that winter occurs at different times of the year in separate hemispheres (due to the tilt of the Earth as it rotates around the sun).

Summarizing and Paraphrasing

Two of the most common ways to organize ideas from a text include paraphrasing and summarizing. Paraphrasing involves taking another's ideas and putting them into one's own words. A paraphrase can involve a single paragraph or encompass the entire main idea of a selection. A summary is used to write the main idea and supporting points of a story in a succinct manner. Summaries are useful when describing the specific points that need to be remembered from an entire story.

Main idea and supporting details

A main idea is the overall premise of a story, or what the author wants the reader to know about their topic in general. In order to show that a main idea is correct, or valid, the author needs to add details that prove their point. Sentences that help to prove the point of the story are called supporting details.

The main idea is often found near the beginning of a story so that the reader knows what the rest of the story will be about. Supporting details need to follow the main idea, since there is nothing to support without a main concept to adhere to! An example of a main idea is: "Giraffes live in the Serengeti of Africa." A supporting detail about giraffes could be: "A giraffe uses its long neck to reach twigs and leaves on trees." The main idea gives the general idea that the text is about giraffes. The supporting detail gives a specific fact about how the giraffes eat.

Example
Read the following sentences. Identify the main idea and supporting detail.
> The new art museum is set to open on September 1st of this year. Paintings from local artists will be displayed for purchase year-round.

A main idea is typically followed by a supporting detail, since a "supporting detail" indicates further information about the main idea. In the example, the reader first learns when the art museum will open, then what will be displayed at the museum. The second sentence gives further information about the art museum.
The main idea of a selection can often be found in the first one to two paragraphs of text. Supporting details come in subsequent paragraphs or further in the same paragraph. When looking for the main idea of a selection, recognize that the main idea will give the reader the main point of the entire story. This allows the reader to know what to expect while reading the rest of the selection.

Fact and opinion

A *fact* is based on information that is presented to the reader from reliable sources. Facts are accurate until proven otherwise. An *opinion* is what the author thinks about a given topic. An opinion is not common knowledge or proven by expert sources, but it is information that the author believes and wants the reader to consider. To distinguish between fact and opinion, a reader needs to look at the type of source that is presenting information, what information backs-up a claim, and whether or not the author may be motivated to have a certain point of view on a given topic. For example, if a panel of scientists has conducted multiple studies on the effectiveness of taking a certain vitamin, the results are more likely to be factual than if a company selling a vitamin claims that taking the vitamin can produce positive effects. The company is motivated to sell its product, while the scientists are using the scientific method to prove a theory. If the author uses words such as "I think…", the statement is an opinion.

Example
Decide whether the following sentence is a fact or opinion. Explain your reasoning.
> My grandmother thinks that writing letters is a better way to communicate than talking on the telephone.

The sentence is a fact; the grandmother does believe that writing letters is better than talking on the telephone. However, the thoughts of the grandmother are her opinion; the sentence as it is presented is stating a fact about the grandmother's beliefs. To give another example, the grandson or granddaughter may believe that writing e-mails is the best way to communicate. The thoughts of the grandson or granddaughter are an opinion, but stating that *the character* feels a certain way about a topic is a fact. The character does feel a certain way about a topic. To write the example sentence as an opinion, the author might state:

- 11 -

Writing letters is a better way to communicate than talking on the telephone. This statement is not proven, it is just an opinion.

Organization of text by readers

Ideas from a text can also be organized using graphic organizers. A spider-map takes a main idea from the story and places it in a bubble, with supporting points branching off the main idea. An outline can be useful for diagramming the main and supporting points of the entire story. A Venn diagram is useful for classifying information as separate or overlapping, whereas a timeline can chronicle the order of events in a story.

Readers often use graphic organizers to recall information from a text. A graphic organizer may be an outline, timeline, mind-map, Venn diagram, or a multitude of other means of organizing information, all of which differ in format. For example, an outline uses Roman numerals, key points, and supporting points to organize information. A timeline is based on a series of dates or times that are an integral part of the story. A Venn diagram is used to compare ideas by placing them in separate circles; sometimes ideas overlap and are placed where the circles converge (come together).
Any type of graphic organizer is a way to simplify information and just take key points from the text. A graphic organizer such as a timeline may have an event listed for a corresponding date on the timeline, whereas an outline may have an event listed under a key point that occurs in the text. Each reader needs to create the type of graphic organizer that works the best for him or her in terms of being able to recall information from a story.

Organization of a sentence

Read the following sentences. Explain how the sentences are organized differently.
1.) Jackie had climbed the mountain once before, on a hot day two summers ago when the air was silent with the wave of heat.
2) Since Jackie had enjoyed her prior climb up the mountain, she decided to hike up the trail once again.

The first sentence uses flashback to refer to an event that occurred in the past. The second sentence uses cause and effect to show why the character made a decision in the story. Note that the first sentence describes what the event was like in the past, while the second sentence gives a reason that the character decided to take an action. An author will often use flashback to present a motivation for a character to take an action in the present or future. The author can also use the passage of time to show chronology of events or foreshadowing to hint at what may occur in the future.

Cause and effect and chronology

Cause and effect is a way authors organize information to show why events occur in a story: one action will lead to the next action, which will lead to a subsequent action. The author uses cause and effect to give the reader information on why each action took place; when the reader goes back to look for a piece of information, they just have to look at the correct point in a story. By using cause and effect, an author can lead the reader through a series of events that are logical.

Chronology places events in the order in which they occur in the story. Time is the key factor in when an event occurs, while the reason it occurs is not as important in terms of organization. Events occur over a short or long period of time, dependent upon the duration of the story. A reader simply needs to refer back to the correct place in time within the story to find a given piece of information within the text.

Synthesizing a text

Synthesizing is similar to summarizing but it takes it one step further. Synthesizing involves taking the main points of a text and comparing it with existing knowledge to create a new idea, perspective, or way of thinking. Instead of using existing knowledge, synthesizing may instead be done by combining the ideas provided in two or three different texts. The reader must make connections between the texts, determine how the ideas fit together, and gather evidence to support the new perspective.

Central Argument

A central argument is the main point of a book or essay. It is the author's opinion and is usually the reason they are writing the book or essay. It can be structured in several different ways including argument by cause and effect, argument by analogy, and argument by authority. When an author uses argument by cause and effect, they are trying to convince the reader that a certain cause will produce a specific effect. An argument by analogy uses perceived similarities as a basis in order to argue for some further similarity that has not yet been observed. Finally, an argument by authority is being used when an author argues for something on the basis of someone's authority. This can be a positive thing when the referenced person's authority involves having a great deal of knowledge on the subject, but would be considered a logical fallacy if the person's authority is unrelated to the subject of the argument.

Rhetorical fallacies

A rhetorical fallacy, or a fallacy of argument, does not allow the open, two-way exchange of ideas upon which meaningful conversations exist. They try to distract the reader with various appeals instead of using logic. Examples of a rhetorical fallacy include, ad hominem, exaggeration, stereotyping, and categorical claims. An ad hominem is an attack on a person's character or personal traits in an attempt to undermine their argument. An exaggeration is the representation of something in an obviously excessive manner. Stereotyping is the thought that all people in a certain group have a certain characteristics or tendencies. A categorical claim is a universal statement about a particular type of thing or person. A categorical claim can be thought of as the verbalization of a stereotype.

Graphical components of a text

The graphical components of a text are the images or figures included in a text to enhance the reader's understanding of what the text is trying to convey. Some common examples of these would be a picture of the engine components in a car owner's manual, or a graph showing the US population at different periods of history in a report on the census.

Text structure

Example 1
Identify the text structure that is used in the following sentences:
> Madison and her brother Jake used to live on a wind-torn island in the Chesapeake Bay. Last year they moved to Baltimore, a city in Maryland. Next summer they plan to visit the island where they grew up.

Chronological order is used as a text structure in the example sentences, as they are organized according to the passage of time. Note that each sentence refers to a point in time. The first sentence refers to where the siblings lived in the past. The second sentence refers to the siblings' move to Baltimore last year. The final sentence refers to what the siblings plan to do in the future. By referring to a specific place in time, the reader can see what occurred in the story during that time period. An author will often use flashback to indicate what happened in the past, and foreshadowing to give the reader a glimpse of what may occur in the future.

Example 2
Identify the text structure that is used in the following sentences:
> Three cousins lived in the same small town. One day the cousins decided to journey together to enter a singing contest across the country. The cousins won the contest and made their hometown fans proud.

The information in the story can be organized according to the passage of time, called chronological order. The story will start based in the cousins' hometown, to give some background on where the cousins come from. Subsequent events in the story will occur over time based on the cousins' motivations due to their background. The story will end by referring back to how far the cousins have come from their small-town roots.
To organize information from the story, a reader can use a graphic organizer. An outline is an excellent way to include the key points of the story, along with supporting points that the author has conveyed. A timeline is another way that a reader can organize the events that occur in the story.

Organization of information within a text

An author may organize information in a chart, a graph, in paragraph format, or as a list. Information may also be presented in a picture or a diagram. The information may be arranged according to the order in which it occurred over time, placed in categories, or it may be arranged in a cause-and-effect relationship. Information can also be presented according to where it occurs in a given space (spatial order), or organized through description. The way an author chooses to organize information is often based on the purpose of information that is being presented, the best way to present given information, and the audience that the information is meant to reach.

Author's point of view

The author will always have a point of view about a story before they draw up a plot line. The author will know what events they want to take place, how they want the characters to interact, and how the story will resolve. An author will also have an opinion on the topic, or series of events, which is presented in the story, based on their own prior experience and beliefs.

Each story can be taken in whatever direction the author wishes. A story will often make sense based on societal norms, but the author can purposely choose to go against these norms to shock the reader. For example, if an author wrote a story about a man who enjoyed living in the bayous of Louisiana, the audience would not expect the character to promptly move to Alaska. Sometimes an author will put a twist in a story just to surprise the reader.

Paraphrasing main point of a sentence

Paraphrase the main point of the following two sentences:
> Emmanuel went swimming in the lake by his house, where the water reached a depth of twenty feet in the middle. He did not venture out more than six feet into the water, however.

When paraphrasing a couple sentences or an entire paragraph, always include the main point of the text being reviewed, this is what the reader needs to know about the text. In the example, the reader needs to know that Emmanuel went swimming in the lake, but not more than six feet out. A paraphrase of the text may include: Emmanuel went swimming six feet out in the lake by his house. That is the main point that the audience needs to know. Recall that a paraphrase is stating the author's ideas in the reader's own words. A summary typically involves including the main points of a longer text, such as a novel or full story.

Drawing a conclusion

<u>Example 1</u>
Draw a conclusion based on the following sentence.
> New Orleans then was a mere huddle of buildings around Jackson Square; but with the purchase of the Louisiana territory from France, and the great influx of American enterprise that characterized the first quarter of the last century, development was working like yeast...

The reader needs to use prior experience and background information to draw an accurate conclusion about the sentence. The sentence describes how New Orleans grew after the "purchase of the Louisiana territory" and how "development was working like yeast". Yeast multiplies rapidly, so the reader can conclude that New Orleans was growing rapidly.

Sometimes interpreting the information in a sentence can be difficult, especially if the reader is unfamiliar with some of the words used in a sentence. Drawing a picture of what is actually happening in the sentence can help, along with looking at the words that the reader does understand in the sentence. By taking a pen or pencil and underlining important information in a sentence, the reader can better understand what the author is trying to say and draw a clearer conclusion from that.

<u>Example 2</u>
Read the following sentence. Draw a conclusion based upon the information presented.
> "A rosy-faced servant-maid opened the door, and smiled as she took the letter which he silently offered."

The reader can conclude, based on the sentence, that the servant-maid is friendly. The words "rosy-faced" and "smiled" lead the reader to this conclusion. People who are friendly are often described as having rosy complexions and smiling as a common sign of pleasantness. The reader can also assume, from the sentence, that the letter does not present any threat or unpleasantness to the servant-maid. The person presenting the letter does not have anything to say upon offering it, so perhaps he is waiting to see how the servant-maid will react.

When interpreting a sentence, always look for key words that describe a character. The author carefully crafts a description of each character, to form a picture in the reader's mind about what the character is like.

Generalization and inference

A *generalization* is an overall conclusion that a reader can draw from a text. For example, if the characters in a text are all expertly fishing from a lobster boat off the coast of Maine, the reader can draw a *generalization* that the characters are experienced Maine fishermen. The details in a story help the reader to make generalizations about characters and the setting of a story. Prior knowledge is often a part of the reader's assumption about information that is presented to them in a story.

An *inference* is a conclusion that the reader draws based upon what is implied in a story. The author may not blatantly state a conclusion, but the reader can come to that conclusion based upon all the information that is presented to them. For example, if the author states that a character prefers indoor activities to outdoor activities, the reader can *infer* that the character would rather read a book outdoors than go on a kayaking trip down a river.

Inductive and deductive organization

Read the following two sentences. Decide whether the ideas are organized inductively or deductively.

> Many canoers use the lake in the summer. Jeff learned how to canoe last summer, and is on his way to the lake now.

The ideas are organized deductively, from general to specific. The idea that "Many canoers use the lake in the summer" is a general idea. The facts that Jeff already knows how to canoe and is headed to the lake are specific to him as a character.

Authors often organize ideas from general to specific or specific to general. If ideas are organized inductively, they are arranged from specific facts to general conclusions. A reader can make a logical assumption about a topic based on the facts that are presented in the text.

Contrasting information

Read the following two sentences. Describe an idea that the author can present in contrast to this information.

> Canadian geese fly south each year to escape the cold of winter. The ponds and lakes that Canadian geese swim on in the summer are often covered with ice in the middle of the winter.

The information being presented by the author is factual. Since the point of the information is to inform the reader, the author can present information about where Canadian geese live in the summer, to contrast how their location of residence looks in the wintertime. To contrast the statement that the lakes are often covered with ice in the winter, the author may state: "The wide open waters where Canadian geese reside in the summer are covered with a range of other wild birds that share the warm, fish- and plant-filled waters of the northern states." By providing contrasting information, an author can provide two different perspectives on the same issue that is being described in a story.

Problem resolution

The term *problem resolution* usually indicates the result of a conflict in a story. Conflict between characters, within a character, or against an external element is necessary in order to have a plot for a story. Without conflict, no events would occur to form the story. A conflict will come to a climax, then conclude in some way. The resolution of a problem may be open-ended, end tragically, or end in a way that is beneficial for all parties involved. The *problem resolution* typically occurs near the end of a story, after the climax and conclusion have occurred. A problem may be resolved by the characters involved within the conflict or by an external event; an upcoming resolution may be foreshadowed in the text, or may be completely unexpected by the reader. If the *problem resolution* is completely unexpected, it is a *twist* in the story.

Literary devices

<u>Example</u>
Read the following sentences and indicate what literary device is used in the text.
> Jamal recalled the first time he had scored in a basketball game; the way the crowd cheered and his feeling of elation came rushing back into his mind

The author of the sentence uses flashback to recall an event in the past. Authors often use literary devices, such as flashback and foreshadowing, to signal what may occur next in a story. For example, if the character Jamal was to score again in the next basketball game, the author may write: "Jamal pictured every time he had scored a basket in the past, to ready himself for scoring more baskets in the next game." The sentence indicates that Jamal will likely score a basket in the next basketball game. By using foreshadowing and flashback, the author can help the reader to predict what will happen in the future based on what happened in the past, all the while hinting as to what will happen in the future.

- 17 -

Reading Practice Test #1

Practice Questions

Questions 1 – 12 pertain to the following passage:

Adventure Land Chase

(1) I had been waiting for Saturday afternoon for what seemed forever. I had the date circled on the calendar in the kitchen, and my mom even let me cross off the days leading up to it. Every day when I would walk into the kitchen, I would see the date circled in a bright green marker and get even more excited.

(2) Saturday was the day that Adventure Land was opening. It is the largest theme park in three states, has massive rollercoaster's that travel at super speed and loop three times, and has a full water park. But it wasn't just the grand opening of Adventure Land about which I was excited. Saturday was also my best friend Riley's birthday, and to celebrate, she was having her birthday party at Adventure Land.

(3) I woke up very early Saturday morning because I could not sleep. I kept thinking about all the rides that we would go on, the games we were going to play, but more than anything, spending time with all of my friends. While I was eating my cereal, my mom packed us a large bag filled with things she said we were going to need at the theme park all day. She packed sunscreen, sunglasses, and water bottles.

I didn't pay attention, because I was still too excited about the biggest rollercoaster, the Slithering Cobra. It was the one that shot up really high and had three loops. It was going to be so much fun!

(4) When we first got to the park, my first thought was that it was a lot bigger than I thought it was going to be. It was huge! I could see the tops of the rollercoasters from the car in the parking lot. Inside, everything was made to look like a jungle. There were lots of different kinds of trees, both real and fake, there were long green vines draped across the park like telephone lines, and the workers were dressed up as if they were going on safari. The park was so big, and there was so much to do, but then I noticed one huge problem. There were so many people in the park. Everywhere I looked, there were more people. I was even bumped a few times while we stood at the entrance.

(5) Riley's mom gave all of us wristbands and said that we had to stay with one of our friends at all times.

(6) "Have a buddy," she said. "If anyone gets lost, come to the food court. We will meet at Lickin' Fried Chicken at one o'clock."

(7) Riley was my buddy, and we immediately ran off to go ride the Slithering Cobra.

(8) "Wait up," Charlotte and Ryan called. "We want to come too!"

(9) We stood in line for the ride for over half an hour. There were so many people, and more people kept coming.

(10) "I'm hot," Riley said.

(11) "This is boring," Ryan complained.

(12) When we finally were at the front of the line, the gates opened, and we were allowed to take our seats. Since it was Riley's birthday, they let us ride in the front seats. The rollercoaster took off really fast and went straight into the air. It stopped at the top of the tracks, and it felt as if we were going to fall out of our seats! The rollercoaster tipped over the edge, and soon we were rushing toward the ground. Riley put her arms up, and we both started screaming. The coaster then went straight up and into the three loops. Before we knew it, we were back at the platform, and the ride was over.

(13) "That was awesome!" Charlotte yelled.

(14) "I want to go again!" Ryan added.

(15) We looked at the line, and it had doubled since we had gotten there.

(16) "Maybe later," I said.

(17) When we got off the ride and were walking toward the arcade, our friend Natalie came running up to us. She looked really worried.

(18) "I've lost him," she said. "I lost George! I wasn't supposed to leave him, but I went to the bathroom and now I can't find him!"

(19) "Did you go to the food court?" Ryan asked.

(20) "Yes, and he wasn't there!" she said.

(21) I didn't know what to do. The park was so big, and there were so many people.

(22) "We will have to retrace your steps," Charlotte said. "Where were you the last time you saw him?"

(23) "In the arcade. Playing skee ball."

(24) We all started running toward the arcade, which was shaped like a giant tiger.

(25) "Make sure we all stay together!" Ryan called.

(26) It was really hot, and the sun was beating down right on our faces. I probably should have thought about putting on my sunglasses, but all I could think of was George.

(27) "Who is George?" Riley asked me while we were running.

(28) "I thought you knew!" I said. "I have no idea. Maybe her brother?"

(29) It felt really nice to be inside of the arcade. It looked just like a jungle, too. I kept thinking there was no way we were going to find him, but we had to try. We ran up a flight of stairs and across the room to the skee ball games.

(30) "There he is!" Natalie pointed forward. We didn't see anything. She ran to one of the alleys and picked up a large stuffed monkey. It was George, the stuffed animal from our homeroom that one student has to take home every weekend and write a story about their adventures. We were bewildered.

(31) "That's the George you were talking about?" Riley whined.

(32) "Of course. Mrs. Miller would have killed me if I lost him! But now I have a great adventure to write about!" she said.

(33) We looked at Natalie and laughed.

(34) "Let's go on another ride," I said, and we all started walking back into the jungle.

1. What is the first reason the narrator gives to explain why she was excited about Saturday?
    a. It was her best friend's birthday
    b. She was going to the beach
    c. Adventure Land was opening
    d. She was going to have the class's stuffed animal

2. In paragraph 3, the author creates a mood of:
    a. Anger
    b. Frustration
    c. Unease
    d. Excitement

3. Paragraphs 1-3 are mainly about:
    a. Why the narrator is looking forward to Saturday
    b. The fun attractions in the narrator's state
    c. Why Adventure Land is fun
    d. Who is coming to the party

4. The narrator uses the words "vines" and "safari" to explain that:
    a. It is hot outside
    b. The theme of the park is the jungle
    c. The park is decorated nicely
    d. The children are not at home

5. Why did Riley's mom ask that every child have a buddy?
    a. So that no one would be lonely
    b. So that no one would get lost
    c. To make the lines for rides move faster
    d. To meet up for lunch

6. Why were the children allowed to ride in the front seat of the rollercoaster?
    a. They had been waiting a really long time
    b. They were in the line for the front seat
    c. They ran and reached the seat the quickest
    d. It was their friend's birthday

7. Why does the narrator discuss the number of people at the park?
    a. To explain why it was important to not get lost
    b. To explain the popularity of the park
    c. To justify her complaints about waiting in line
    d. To explain that it was hot

8. What is the children's main conflict in this selection?
    a. Beating the crowds to get in line for the best ride
    b. Wearing sunscreen
    c. Trying to find a friend they think is lost
    d. Meeting their parents for lunch

9. Why does Ryan ask Natalie if she has been to the food court?
    a. He is hungry and wants to know if the food is good
    b. It is where they were supposed to go if they were lost
    c. It is time to meet up for lunch
    d. He thinks she should talk to one of the parents

10. In paragraph 30, what does the word bewildered mean?
    a. Happy
    b. Upset
    c. Confused
    d. Numb

11. How is the conflict of the story resolved?
    a. The children find George
    b. The lines on the rides become shorter
    c. The children don't care about a stuffed animal
    d. The children leave the park

12. Why are the children surprised at the end of the story?
    a. That there were no lines in the arcade
    b. Adventure Land was not as much fun as they thought
    c. Natalie didn't have a buddy
    d. George was a stuffed animal

Questions 13 – 22 pertain to the following passage:

Happily Never After

(1) The tragic story of two star-crossed lovers was first brought to attention in William Shakespeare's play, Romeo and Juliet.

(2) The entire plot of the play is explained in the prologue. It is stated that there are two households of equal status in Verona, Italy. There is an ancient feud between the two families that has progressed into the younger generations, meaning the fight between the parents has now become the fight between the parents' children. The narrator continues, saying, "A pair of star-crossed lovers take their life" and in doing so, end their parents' feud. Romeo and Juliet, a child of each household, fall in love, but cannot live happily together because of the feud. The feud is ended, but it is an act that only the death of these children could make happen.

(3) The majority of stories that audiences enjoy have a happy ending. From childhood, people have grown up with the expectation of an ending that comes with the phrase, "And they lived happily ever after." It is interesting that the story of Romeo and Juliet, a famous tragedy, has extreme popularity and interest among both storytellers and audiences. This raises the question of fascination with tragedy.

(4) In the last act of the play, Juliet has faked her death to escape marriage to another man. A message is supposed to be sent to Romeo explaining that she is alive with a plan for their escape. The message, however, does not reach Romeo. In his despair that he has lost his love, he comes to Juliet's side,

drinks poison, and dies. Moments later, Juliet wakes up to find Romeo dead. In her grief, she takes his dagger and kills herself.

(5) Within the prologue, the first moments of the play, the audience is told that the main characters die. It is an interesting way of storytelling. The plot has been ruined, and there is no suspense. The audience is told that Romeo and Juliet die, and in doing so, end their parents' feud. The audience, however, remains, and watches the events take place, even though they know the ending and that it will not be happy.

(6) It is therefore logical to assume that audiences want to believe that a story will end happily, even though they are given evidence that it will not. Audiences will watch the entire play, hoping that something will be done so that the lovers can be saved. And yet, as the prologue stated, the message is not delivered, and the only way that Romeo and Juliet can be together is in death. Their deaths had to take place before the ancient feud would end.

(7) The theme of tragic love has been repeated throughout literary history, although perhaps not brought to the extreme of Romeo and Juliet. Although audiences enjoy stories with a happy ending, the popularity of tragic themes proves that audiences also enjoy stories that do not end happily. It is the hope for happiness that gives tragedies strength, and the hope that things will end differently.

13. Which of these sentences is an opinion?
    a. The feud is ended, but it is an act that only the death of their children could make happen
    b. Moments later, Juliet wakes up to find Romeo dead
    c. Audiences will watch the entire play, hoping that something will be done so that the lovers can be saved
    d. It is stated that there are two households of equal status in Verona, Italy

14. What occurs during the first moments of the play?
    a. Romeo dies
    b. There is a fight
    c. Romeo and Juliet share a kiss
    d. The prologue

15. Paragraph 2 helps the reader to understand:
    a. The characters in Romeo and Juliet
    b. The conflict and plot in Romeo and Juliet
    c. The mood and tone in Romeo and Juliet
    d. The theme of Romeo and Juliet

16. What does the word feud mean in paragraph 5?
    a. Fight
    b. Happiness
    c. Sadness
    d. Wealth

17. What is the author's main argument?
    a. Romeo and Juliet is a great play
    b. Audiences will still hope a tragic story will end happily
    c. Tragedies are not as good as stories that have a happy ending
    d. Prologues should not ruin the story

18. What does the word evidence mean in paragraph 6?
    a. Hope
    b. Questions
    c. Proof
    d. Sadness

19. Why does the author use the phrase, "And they lived happily ever after"?
    a. To explain that most audiences enjoy stories with a happy ending
    b. To explain the ending of Romeo and Juliet
    c. To explain why happy endings are not as good as tragic endings
    d. To explain how to end a story

20. The author explains that Romeo believes Juliet to be dead because:
    a. He watched her take his dagger
    b. She drank poison
    c. She was ill on her wedding day
    d. He never received the message explaining that she faked her death

21. Why does the author think that the prologue in Romeo and Juliet is "an interesting way of storytelling"?
    a. The prologue explains that the play is a tragedy
    b. The prologue explains how the story will end
    c. The prologue is very long
    d. The prologue asks the audience a question

22. Why, according to the prologue and author, are Romeo and Juliet's deaths necessary?
    a. To make the play a tragedy
    b. To show the dangers of poison
    c. To end their parents' feud
    d. To earn more money and power

Questions 23 – 25 pertain to the following poem:

The Window

Rain spilled like rivers—
the wind whispered
against the window.

Steam rose from the cup
in swirls;
white against the darkness.

Nestled in the warmth
of blankets and tea,
Mother listened to the sounds
knocking outside the window.

23. In the poem, "The Window," what is an example of personification?
    a. Spilled
    b. Nestled
    c. Whispered
    d. Rose

24. In the poem, "The Window," the author uses a simile to compare:
    a. Steam and swirls
    b. Blankets and tea
    c. White and darkness
    d. Rain and rivers

25. In the poem, "The Window," what is a proper noun?
    a. Nestled
    b. Mother
    c. Rain
    d. darkness

Questions 26 – 33 pertain to the following passage:

Musically Inclined

(1) Gibson thought, at least, that it could have been worse. His parents could have named him Fender, given him the middle name Les Paul, or worse yet, Stratocaster. This was a small comfort to him as he reminded himself that he really never had a chance. It was not he who chose the music. He was born into it, and even named after one of the most famous guitars. It was like the music had found him.
(2) Gibson could not remember a time when he did not know how to play music. His mother was a singer when she was younger, and his father played the lead guitar in the band Mookie Harper. Growing up, he learned to read music at the same time he learned to read words. Music felt as natural to him as walking and was a big part of his life.

- 24 -

(3) There were many instruments in Gibson's house, and over the years, he had learned how to play most of them. He started with a piano when he was very young, moved to the harmonica and drums when he was a bit older, and had just begun learning how to play the violin. But Gibson's favorite instrument was the one he had been playing the longest: his father's Gibson Les Paul guitar.

(4) At school, Gibson felt lonely most days. His family had just moved from Seattle, and the other kids at school thought it was weird that he carried a violin case to school for his fourth period music class. At his old school, he was in the school band, and had a lot of friends who enjoyed playing music with him.

(5) "Why would you play the violin?" Joe asked as he snickered in his chair. "Only girls play that. I bet it was the only thing you could learn," he laughed. The rest of the class laughed behind him.

(6) Gibson sat in his chair and rolled his eyes. He thought that this kid obviously didn't know anything about music, because the violin was one of the most challenging instruments to learn. He left the case on the floor by his chair and waited for his second period history class to begin.

(7) The teacher walked into the classroom pushing a cart. Gibson immediately sat up in his chair. He knew exactly what was in the cases and smiled.

(8) "I was able to borrow these from the music section of the museum to show you today," Ms. Conway said. "Can anyone tell me what these are?" she asked.

(9) "They are guitars, Ms. Conway. Duh," Joe, a boy in the back of the room, said. The class laughed.

(10) Ms. Conway squinted her eyes at Joe. "He is half right," she said. "These are in fact guitars. But can anyone tell me what kind of guitars they are?" She looked around the room. Everyone sat still.

(11) "The one on the right is a 1958 Gibson Les Paul," Gibson said out of the silence. "And the one of the left is a vintage Fender Stratocaster from 1954. Oh, and they are electric guitars," he said.

(12) The class looked at Gibson and stared in silence. Ms. Conway clapped her hands together. "Wow! You're right, Gibson. Great job!"

(13) "How'd you know that?" a girl asked behind him.

(14) "My dad has both of them," he said. "And I've been playing them since I was little."

(15) "You can play the guitar?" Joe laughed. "Yeah right! You play the violin!" He looked around, but no one else was laughing.

(16) "Would you like to play something?" Ms. Conway asked. Gibson looked down at his feet. He didn't know what to say. He just wanted to stay in his seat and have no one look at him.

(17) But then he thought of his dad and smiled. "I'll play the Les Paul," he said. "It's my favorite."

(18) He walked toward the front of the class and picked up the guitar. He played the opening notes of "Gone into the Sun." It was his favorite Mookie Harper song. All of the children sat in awe as they watched him play, and when he was done, they all started clapping and cheering.

(19) "Maybe I'll start playing the violin," the boy next to him said. "If it will get me to play a guitar like that!"

26. Paragraphs 1 through 3 are mainly about:
     a. How music has inspired Gibson's family and his life
     b. How Gibson will be in a band one day
     c. How Gibson wanted to be named after a Fender guitar
     d. Why Gibson is moving schools

27. This story is told in what point of view?
     a. First-person limited
     b. First-person omniscient
     c. Third-person omniscient
     d. Third-person limited

28. Why did the narrator include the detail that the family was from Seattle?
     a. To show why the family loves music
     b. To show that Gibson was a new student
     c. To show that the family moves a lot because of the father's band
     d. To show that the family is on vacation

29. What does Gibson mean when he assumes that he "never really had a chance?"
     a. That he was destined to play music because of his family and his name
     b. That he was never going to be good at playing the violin
     c. That he was never going to be popular at school
     d. That he is going to be in a band one day like his father

30. What instrument had Gibson been playing the longest?
     a. Violin
     b. Harmonica
     c. Les Paul guitar
     d. Fender Stratocaster guitar

31. In paragraph 16, why did Gibson want to sit in his seat?
     a. He did not like the guitar and did not want to play it
     b. He did not want the attention of the other children to be on him
     c. He wanted to play the violin instead
     d. He thought the guitar was too old to play

32. The author arranges this selection by:
     a. Explaining how Gibson grew to like to play the violin
     b. Showing how Gibson taught his classmates how to play guitar
     c. Listing why the children laughed at Gibson
     d. Describing how his love for music helped Gibson be himself at school

33. How is the internal conflict in the story resolved?
     a. Gibson is himself and is liked by his classmates
     b. Gibson decides not to play in front of everyone
     c. Gibson decides to start a band with people in his class
     d. Gibson plays a song for his dad

Questions 34 – 42 pertain to the following essay that Timmy has written on why he feels books will soon be a thing of the past:

The Inventions of Technology

(1) Stories have been a part of the world since the beginning of recorded time. For centuries before the invention of the printing press, stories of the world were passed down to generations through oral tradition. With the invention of the printing press, which made written material available to wide ranges of audiences, books were mass-produced and introduced into greater society.

(2) For the last several centuries, books have been at the forefront of education and entertainment. With the invention of the Internet, reliance on books for information quickly changed. Soon, almost everything that anyone needed to know could be accessed through the Internet. Large printed volumes of encyclopedias became unnecessary as all of the information was easily available on the Internet.

(3) Despite the progression of the Internet, printed media was still very popular in the forms of both fiction and non-fiction books. While waiting for an appointment, enduring a several-hour flight, or relaxing before sleep, books have been a reliable and convenient source of entertainment, and one that society has not been willing to give up.

(4) With the progression and extreme convenience of technology, printed books are going to soon become a thing of the past. Inventions such as the iPad from Macintosh and the Kindle have made the need for any kind of printed media unnecessary. With a rechargeable battery, a large screen, and the ability to have several books saved on file, electronic options will soon take over and society will no longer see printed books.

(5) Although some people may say that the act of reading is not complete without turning a page, sliding a finger across the screen or pressing a button to read more onto the next page is just as satisfying to the reader. The iPad and Kindle are devices that have qualities similar to a computer and can be used for so much more than just reading. These devices are therefore better than books because they have multiple uses.

(6) In a cultural society that is part of the world and due to a longstanding tradition, stories will always be an important way to communicate ideas and provide information and entertainment. Centuries ago, stories could only be remembered and retold through speech. Printed media changed the way the world communicated and was connected, and now, as we move forward with technology, it is only a matter of time before we must say goodbye to the printed past and welcome the digital and electronic future.

34. What is the main argument of this essay?
    a. iPad and Kindles are easier to read than books
    b. The printing press was a great invention
    c. The Internet is how people receive information
    d. Technology will soon replace printed material

35. What is the main purpose of paragraph 1?
    a. To explain oral tradition
    b. To explain the importance of the printing press
    c. To explain the progression of stories within society
    d. To introduce the essay

36. What does the word enduring mean in paragraph 3?
    a. Quitting
    b. Undergo
    c. Sleeping
    d. Thriving

37. According to the essay, what was the first way that stories were communicated and passed down?
    a. Oral tradition
    b. Printed books
    c. Technology
    d. Hand writing

38. According to the essay, what changed the reliance on books?
    a. Inventions such as the iPad
    b. The printing press
    c. The Internet
    d. Volumes of encyclopedias

39. Which of the following statements is an opinion?
    a. Despite the progression of the Internet, printed media was still very popular in the forms of both fiction and non-fiction books
    b. Although some people may say that the act of reading is not complete without turning a page, sliding a finger across the screen or pressing a button to read more onto the next page is just as satisfying to the reader
    c. With the invention of the Internet, reliance on books for information quickly changed
    d. Stories have been a part of the world since the beginning of recorded time

40. What is a secondary argument the author makes?
    a. Devices such as the iPad or Kindle are better than books because they have multiple uses
    b. Books are still important to have while waiting for an appointment or taking a flight
    c. Printed encyclopedias are still used and more convenient that using the Internet
    d. With technology, there will soon be no need for stories

41. How is the essay organized?
    a. The author explains details as to why he wants to have an iPad
    b. The author explains how stories eventually let into oral tradition
    c. The author explains technology to explain why books are not needed
    d. The author explains the history of stories within society and the ways they progress with time

42. Which of the following statements is not an example of a categorical claim?
   a. With a rechargeable battery, a large screen, and the ability to have several books saved on file, electronic options will soon take over and society will no longer see printed books.
   b. Soon, almost everything that anyone needed to know could be accessed through the Internet.
   c. The iPad and Kindle are devices that have qualities similar to a computer and can be used for so much more than just reading.
   d. With the progression and extreme convenience of technology, printed books are going to soon become a thing of the past.

Questions 43 – 50 pertain to the following passage:

The Educational Market Town

(1) Aberystwyth is a market town on the West Coast of Wales within the United Kingdom. A market town refers to European areas that have the right to have markets, which differentiates it from a city or village. The town is located where two rivers meet, the River Ystwyth and River Rheidol and is the best known as an educational center, housing an established university since 1872.

(2) The town is situated between North Wales and South Wales, and is a large vacation destination as well as tourist attraction. Constitution Hill is a hill on the north end of Aberystwyth, which provides excellent views of Cardigan Bay and which is supported by the Aberystwyth Electric Cliff Railway. Although Aberystwyth is known as a modern Welsh town, it is home to several historic buildings, such as the remnants of a castle.

(3) Although there are several grocery, clothing, sporting goods, and various other miscellaneous shops, Aberystwyth is best known for its educational services. Aberystwyth University, formerly known as University College Wales, as well as the National Library of Wales, which is the legal deposit library for Wales and which houses all Welsh publications, are both located within Aberystwyth. The two main languages traditionally spoken in Aberystwyth are English and Welsh. With local live music, arts center, and educational opportunities in gorgeous scenery, Aberystwyth is a hidden luxury within the United Kingdom.

43. Where is Aberystwyth located?
   a. England
   b. Ireland
   c. Scotland
   d. Wales

44. What is the purpose of this essay?
   a. To explain that the university was established in 1872
   b. To explain the legal deposit library in Wales
   c. To provide a portrait of a town
   d. To explain the views in Aberystwyth

45. What does the word situated mean in paragraph 2?
   a. located
   b. fighting
   c. luxurious
   d. hidden

46. Which of the following statements is an opinion?
   a. Although Aberystwyth is known as a modern Welsh town, it is home to several historic buildings, such as the remnants of a castle
   b. With local live music, arts center, and educational opportunities in gorgeous scenery, Aberystwyth is a hidden luxury within the United Kingdom
   c. The two main languages traditionally spoken in Aberystwyth are English and Welsh
   d. Aberystwyth is a market town on the West Coast of Wales within the United Kingdom

47. How many languages are traditionally spoken in Aberystwyth?
   a. One
   b. Two
   c. Three
   d. More than three

48. What makes Aberystwyth a market town?
   a. It is a city
   b. It is a village
   c. It has the right to have a market
   d. There are markets in town every day

49. What is Constitution Hill supported by?
   a. Cardigan Bay
   b. The ocean
   c. North Wales
   d. Aberystwyth Electric Cliff Railway

50. What is Aberystwyth best known as?
   a. An educational center
   b. A market town
   c. A music center
   d. A hiking center

Answers and Explanations

TEKS Standard §110.19(b)(6)
1. C: In the first sentence in paragraph 2, it is stated that "Saturday was the day Adventure Land was opening." In paragraph 1, the narrator explains that she is excited and later states that Saturday is her friend's birthday, but the first reason given is that Adventure Land is opening.

TEKS Standard §110.19(b)(8)
2. D: The narrator provides many examples of her excitement throughout paragraph 3, such as that she could not sleep and was not listening to her mom because she was thinking about all of the fun things she was going to do.

TEKS Standard §110.19(b)(6)
3. A: The narrator begins the essay by stating that she was looking forward to Saturday, and the following paragraphs explain why. Although other elements are explained, the main focus is why Saturday is exciting.

TEKS Standard §110.19(b)(8)
4. B: Words like "vines" and "safari" bring about images that reflect the jungle. The narrator explained that the amusement park was decorated in the theme of the jungle and used these words to help create the image.

TEKS Standard §110.19(b)(6)
5. B: Paragraph 5 explains that Riley's mom wanted the children to stay with their buddies, and in paragraph 6, Riley's mom tells the children what to do if they get lost. If the children stayed with their buddy, there was less of a chance of someone getting lost.

TEKS Standard §110.19(b)(6)
6. D: In paragraph 12, the narrator states that since it was her friend's birthday, they were allowed to ride in the front seats.

TEKS Standard §110.19(b)(8)
7. A: The narrator mentions being lost several times throughout the essay, and the central conflict is when the children think someone is lost. The narrator explains that there are many people in the park to create an image that it would be easy to get lost, which would be bad.

TEKS Standard §110.19(b)(6)(B)
8. C: Paragraphs 17-26 explain the conflict the children have when they think someone is lost. They become very worried and try to find George. The narrator mentions earlier that Riley's mother did not want anyone lost, and so the conflict is to find the lost friend.

TEKS Standard §110.19(b)(6)
9. B: Natalie was with George and the children assume that she was his buddy. In paragraph 6, Riley's mother states that if anyone gets lost, they should go to the food court. Since George is lost, the children assume he must have gone to the food court.

- 31 -

TEKS Standard §110.19(b)(2)(A) and (2)(B)

10. C: Bewildered means to become confused. Since the children were expecting George to be a person, they were confused to find a stuffed animal.

TEKS Standard §110.19(b)(6)(B)

11. A: The conflict of the story is trying to find George, who is lost. The conflict is resolved when George is found.

TEKS Standard §110.19(b)(6)

12. D: The children were worried because they thought of one their friends was lost. They were surprised to discover that they had been searching for a stuffed animal and not a person.

TEKS Standard §110.19(b)(10)(B)

13. C: The author assumes that audiences will hope the lovers can be saved. This is not a fact. Choices A, B, and D are all facts that are supported by information in the play.

TEKS Standard §110.19(b)(10)

14. D: Paragraph 5 states that the prologue is in the first moments of the play.

TEKS Standard §110.19(b)(10)

15. B: Paragraph 2 explains all of the information that is in the prologue, and the author says that the prologue provides the plot of the play. The conflict is also explained in discussing the feud between the families.

TEKS Standard §110.19(b)(2)(A) and (2)(B)

16. A: Feud means disagreement, argument, or fight.

TEKS Standard §110.19(b)(10)(A)

17. B: Paragraphs 6 and 7 explain that the author believes that even though they watch a play with the understanding that it will be tragic, they continue to watch it because they hope it will end happily.

TEKS Standard §110.19(b)(2)(A) and (2)(B)

18. C: Evidence means providing help to reveal truth or proof. The prologue provides evidence that the play will not end happily.

TEKS Standard §110.19(b)(10)(A)

19. A: In paragraph 3, the author states that most people expect and enjoy a happy ending as they have grown up with stories that end happily with the phrase, "And they lived happily ever after."

TEKS Standard §110.19(b)(10)(A)

20. D: In paragraph 4, the author explains that Juliet faked her death and that Romeo does not receive the message.

TEKS Standard §110.19(b)(10)(A)

21. B: In paragraph 5, the author explains that it is interesting to explain at the beginning of the play that Romeo and Juliet die and that their deaths end their parents' feud.

TEKS Standard §110.19(b)(10)(A)

22. C: In paragraph 2, the narrator explains that the prologue states that Romeo and Juliet take their lives and in doing so, end their parents' feud.

TEKS Standard §110.19(b)(8)

23. C: Personification is giving human traits to non-human objects. Wind, an object and not a person, cannot whisper.

TEKS Standard §110.19(b)(8)

24. D: A simile compares two things by using the words "like" or "as". The author compares the rain to rivers by using the word, "like".

TEKS Standard §110.19(b)(4)

25. B: "Mother" is a proper noun because it is referring to a unique name, rather than a common noun. "Mother" in the poem is used as a name, which is why it is capitalized.

TEKS Standard §110.19(b)(6)

26. A: Paragraph 1 discusses how Gibson was named and that he was born into music. Paragraph 2 discusses music within his parent's lives. Paragraph 3 discusses how he came to play instruments.

TEKS Standard §110.19(b)(6)(C)

27. D: The story is third-person limited as it is not told in the first-person, by Gibson or any other character, and the narrator only knows the thoughts and feelings of one character, Gibson.

TEKS Standard §110.19(b)(6)

28. B: Paragraph 4 states that Gibson's family had just moved from Seattle, which explains that he is a new student in the school.

TEKS Standard §110.19(b)(6)

29. A: Paragraph 1 discusses music in Gibson's life and the fact that he was born into music through his family and even his name. He thinks that it was the music that chose him, and because of this, he "never really had a chance" to not have music be very involved in his life.

TEKS Standard §110.19(b)(6)

30. C: In paragraph 3, it is stated that Gibson's favorite instrument was also the one he had been playing the longest, his father's Gibson Les Paul guitar.

TEKS Standard §110.19(b)(6)

31. B: The narrator explains that Gibson wanted to stay in his seat and have no one look at him. He did not want the attention of the other children.

TEKS Standard §110.19(b)(6)(B)

32. D: From the beginning of the essay, the narrator states that music was always a part of Gibson's life and helped shaped his interests. The essay moves into discussing Gibson at a new school, and eventually how his love of music helps him to be himself at school.

TEKS Standard §110.19(b)(6)(B)

33. A: The conflict in the story is that as a new student, Gibson is teased by his fellow classmates. By showing his love of music as well as his talent, Gibson is himself and is liked by his classmates.

TEKS Standard §110.19(b)(11)(A)

34. D: The main argument is stated in paragraph 4: "With the progression and extreme convenience of technology, printed books are going to soon become a thing of the past."

TEKS Standard §110.19(b)(11)(A)

35. C: Paragraph 1 explains how stories have progressed, beginning with oral tradition and past the invention of the printing press. In context with the rest of the essay, this paragraph is important in explaining how stories progress and are provided within society.

TEKS Standard §110.19(b)(2)(A) and (2)(B)

36. B: Enduring means to put up with something unpleasant. Within the sentence, the phrase, "enduring a several hour flight," the word enduring, means to undergo.

TEKS Standard §110.19(b)(11)

37. A: In paragraph 1, it is stated that oral tradition was the main medium for storytelling before the invention of the printing press.

TEKS Standard §110.19(b)(11)

38. C: In paragraph 2, it is stated that reliance on books for information was changed with the invention of the Internet.

TEKS Standard §110.19(b)(10)(B)

39. B: It is not a fact that "sliding a finger across the screen or pressing a button to move onto the next page is just as satisfying to the reader." Satisfaction is not something universal that can be proven for every reader. This statement is an opinion.

TEKS Standard §110.19(b)(11) and (11)(A)

40. A: The author makes the argument in paragraph 5 that devices such as the iPad and Kindle are "therefore better than books because they have multiple uses."

TEKS Standard §110.19(b)(11) and (11)(A)

41. D: In the beginning of the essay, the author explains how stories were passed through oral tradition. This was changed by the printing press, which is becoming less important with technology and the invention of the Internet and devices such as the iPad and Kindle.

TEKS Standard §110.19(b)(10)(B)

42. C: A categorical claim is an arguable understanding of facts, rather than an absolute fact. The statement regarding the qualities of the iPad and Kindle is the only statement that is a fact.

TEKS Standard §110.19(b)(10)

43. D: Paragraph 1 states that Aberystwyth is located on the West Coast of Wales.

TEKS Standard §110.19(b)(10)(A)

44. C: The essay provides information on various aspects of the town of Aberystwyth, providing a portrait of the town as a whole.

TEKS Standard §110.19(b)(2)(A) and (B)

45. A: Situated means to be placed in a certain location.

TEKS Standard §110.19(b)(10)(B)

46. B: In an essay that is factual, proclaiming that the scenery is "gorgeous" or that a town is a "hidden luxury" is an opinion.

TEKS Standard §110.19(b)(10)

47. B: Paragraph 3 states that two main languages are traditionally spoken in Aberystwyth.

TEKS Standard §110.19(b)(10)

48. C: Paragraph 1 states, "A market town refers to European areas that have the right to have markets, which differentiates it from a city or village."

TEKS Standard §110.19(b)(10)

49. D: Paragraph 2 states, "Constitution Hill is a hill on the north end of Aberystwyth, which provides excellent views of Cardigan Bay and which is supported by the Aberystwyth Electric Cliff Railway."

TEKS Standard §110.19(b)(10)

50. A: Paragraph 1 explains that Aberystwyth is best known as an education center, and this is repeated in paragraph 3, which states that Aberystwyth is best known for its educational services.

Reading Practice Test #2

Practice Questions

Questions 1 – 12 pertain to the following passage:
Summer's Heat

(1) I remember the day as if it were yesterday. It was Saturday afternoon and cloudless. The sun beat down upon my face, even through the chain link fenced dugout. It was so hot that I could feel my skin burning, and I was sweating, even though I wasn't on the field. I sat on the bench with a jug of water at my feet and a fistful of sunflower seeds. We were losing, three to one. I looked at our right fielder, Johnny, who was fanning his face with his glove as he was getting ready for the play.

(2) The ball was hit to the third basemen, and he got the last out of the inning at first base. The team ran into a huddle, and our coach told us to keep our eye on the ball. "Concentrate," he said.

(3) Philip hit the ball to the fence and was stopped on second base by the coaches. We were all shouting and very happy with his double. The next batter bunted the ball to the pitcher, and moved Philip to third base. Johnny then came to the plate and hit a double. Philip scored, and we were one run away from tying the game.

(4) "Max!" the coach shouted.

(5) I turned my head and was shocked to see that I wasn't imagining things. Coach was pointing right at me.

(6) "You're up," he said.

(7) I threw my sunflower seeds to the ground, stuffed my helmet onto my head, and grabbed my favorite bat. I took two practice swings and was ready for the pitcher.

(8) I hit two foul balls over the side fences. They were hard, and flew for a long time before ever hitting the ground. I was going to do it. I was going to get Johnny to home plate. I just needed one good pitch.

(9) The pitcher looked down at his feet and then stared into my eyes. I stared back. It was like there was no one else on the field. It was just us. He started his windup, and I dug my feet into the ground and adjusted my grip on the bat. The ball game in and I swung at hard as I could.

(10) I was confused. I didn't feel anything.

(11) "Strike three!" the umpire yelled behind me.

(12) I was out.

(13) Bradley came up after me and we ended up losing the game, three to two.

(14) The coaches told us we played a good game. They said that it was a team effort and that we should be proud of ourselves. My mom told me it was not my fault. "It was no one's fault," she said. "It is just a game."

(15) But it was not just a game to me. I felt like I had let everyone down and disappointed all of my teammates. It was the last game of the season, and we lost.

- 36 -

(16) I decided at that moment to spend my summer vacation training. I was going to do nothing but practice baseball. I spent two weeks outside, with just my baseball bat and a bucket of balls. I hit until it was dark and my mom forced me to come inside and eat dinner. When I asked her if we could install some lights into the backyard so that I could see and practice more, she looked at me with a very stern face and said the most horrible sentence.

(17) "No more baseball for the rest of the summer."

(18) My heart dropped. I felt sick to my stomach and filled with anger.

(19) "How can you do this to me?" I shouted back.

(20) "There is more to life than baseball," she said. "I want you to enjoy spending the summer playing with your friends."

(21) She then grounded me for the weekend for shouting at her.

(22) After a few days without baseball, I realized how fun it was to be a regular kid and spend time with my friends, swimming in the pool, fishing in the lake, and climbing trees. Once, someone suggested we play some baseball, and we gathered some of our friends together and played a game in the park. We didn't keep score, and had fun just playing. It was a great summer.

(23) When baseball season came around again, I played center field. My first time up to bat, I smiled. I was having fun. The pitch came and I swung hard. The ball landed on the other side of the fence, and I ran around the bases to cheers after hitting my first homerun.

1. What image is created in paragraph 1?
    a. Saturday is boring
    b. Baseball players are lazy
    c. It is hot outside
    d. The month of July

2. Why does the narrator include the detail that Johnny was "fanning his face with his glove"?
    a. To demonstrate that Johnny is lazy
    b. To explain why Max should be playing instead of Johnny
    c. To show that Johnny is bored
    d. To provide another image that it is hot outside

3. Why did Max's mom tell him no more baseball?
    a. She wanted him to have fun and not worry about practice
    b. She did not want to install lights
    c. She was afraid he was going to get hurt
    d. She did not want him to be a baseball player anymore

4. What is the point of view of the essay?
    a. First-person omniscient
    b. First-person limited
    c. Third-person omniscient
    d. Third-person limited

5. Why did Max think he was imagining things?
    a. It was so hot outside
    b. He could not believe his team was losing
    c. The coach was calling his name to come into the game to bat
    d. He was surprised to see that Philip scored

6. In paragraph 9, the author creates the mood of:
    a. Tension
    b. Anger
    c. Comfort
    d. Sadness

7. Why was Max confused after he swung in paragraph 10?
    a. It was his first swing
    b. He did not hit the ball
    c. He hit the ball far
    d. He thought he had another opportunity to hit

8. Why did Max want to practice baseball all summer?
    a. He was bored
    b. All of his friends were gone
    c. He was mad at his team for losing the game
    d. He was mad at himself and wanted to get better at baseball

9. What does the word install mean in paragraph 16?
    a. Break
    b. Turn on
    c. Put in
    d. Make bigger

10. What does the word stern mean in paragraph 16?
    a. Soft
    b. Severe
    c. Happy
    d. Unhappy

11. What is the main conflict of this essay?
    a. Max balancing having fun with his love of baseball
    b. Max striking out
    c. Max's team losing the game
    d. Max's mom forbidding baseball

12. How is the conflict resolved?
    a. Max gets better at baseball
    b. Max gets a new baseball team
    c. Max's mom lets him practice more
    d. Max realizing that baseball is a game and should be fun

Questions 13 – 23 pertain to the following passage:
Eating at the Theater

(1) Last Saturday night my family went to go see a movie, and I was introduced to an amazing movie theater, the Alamo Drafthouse Cinema. The Alamo Drafthouse Cinema is like no other movie theater experience. For one thing, no one under the age of eighteen is allowed into the theater without a parent or guardian, no matter the rating of the film. The most incredible part of the Alamo Drafthouse Cinema, and what makes it so unique, is that you get to order an entire meal, get it delivered, and eat it all while watching the movie.

(2) The Alamo Drafthouse Cinema originated in Austin, Texas, and started out as a single screen theater. The unique concept caught a lot of attention and popularity, and soon, the theater was home to film premiers, and even hosted local and visiting filmmakers. In the years since its inception, the Alamo Drafthouse Cinema has grown into a larger franchise. There are currently five locations in Austin, and the theater has expanded into Houston, San Antonio, and Winchester, Virginia.

(3) When we first walked into the lobby, I noticed the decorations on the walls. They were very intricate and three-dimensional, and made me feel like I was a part of the theater, or maybe a part of the movie. When we were able to get inside of the theater, I was surprised to see that it looked like a normal movie theater expect for a large tabletop that extended across the length of every aisle of seats.

(4) I ordered a meal of chicken tenders and French fries, and my sister ordered a hamburger. We were not surprised to find that the food was delicious. Everything about the theater was great. The members of the staff inside of the lobby were very friendly, and our waiter was very nice. Throughout the movie, he walked as quickly as he could so that he would not disrupt the movie. My entire family had a wonderful time at the movies on Saturday, and we have all decided to go back again, to the Alamo Drafthouse Cinema.

13. Which of the following statements is an opinion?
    a. The Alamo Drafthouse Cinema originated in Austin, Texas, and started out as a single screen theater.
    b. For one thing, no one under the age of eighteen is allowed into the theater without a parent or guardian, no matter the rating of the film.
    c. Everything about the theater was great.
    d. In the years since its inception, the Alamo Drafthouse Cinema has grown into a larger franchise.

14. What does the word inception mean in paragraph 2?
    a. Creation
    b. Failure
    c. Progress
    d. Construction

15. Why does the narrator say that the Alamo Drafthouse Cinema is "like no other movie theater experience"?
    a. The movies are not shown at other theaters
    b. The lobby is better
    c. The food tastes better
    d. No one under 18 can be admitted without a parent or guardian

16. Where did the Alamo Drafthouse Cinema originate?
    a. Virginia
    b. San Antonio
    c. Austin
    d. Houston

17. What does the word intricate mean in paragraph 3?
    a. Sturdy
    b. Detailed
    c. Flat
    d. Expensive

18. Why did the narrator say that she felt a part of the theater?
    a. The lobby had three-dimensional decorations
    b. The large tabletop was familiar
    c. The service was excellent
    d. The narrator could order a meal

19. Why was the narrator not surprised that the food was delicious?
    a. Because the narrator ordered normally good tasting food
    b. Because the movie was really good
    c. Because food tastes better when watching a movie
    d. Because everything at the theater was good

20. What did the waiter do so that he did not disrupt the movie?
    a. He spoke quietly
    b. He only delivered food in slow parts of the movie
    c. He walked as quickly as he could
    d. He waited until the movie was over

21. The narrator said that the inside of the theater looked like a normal movie theater except:
    a. There were three-dimensional decorations on the wall
    b. There were no lights
    c. There were round tables all around
    d. There was a tabletop that extended across the aisle

22. In what order is this essay organized?
    a. A review of the film and experience
    b. An introduction, history of the theater, and description of experience
    c. An introduction, description of the physical theater, and dislikes
    d. A detailed explanation of the history of the theater

23. How many cities have at least one Alamo Drafthouse Cinema?
    a. Four
    b. Three
    c. Five
    d. One

Questions 24 – 36 pertain to the following passage:

The Royal Scenery

(1) To celebrate their fifteenth wedding anniversary, my parents decided to take our family on vacation to London. This was the first time that I had ever been out of the country, and I was very excited. While in London, we discovered some really cool places, but my favorite was The Regent's Park in the City of Westminster in central London.

(2) The Regent's Park, to which most people refer to as "Regent's Park," is one of the eight Royal Parks in Greater London. A Royal Park is land that was once owned by the royal monarchy, or crown, of the United Kingdom. A monarchy is a form of government where a monarch acts as the head of state. Currently, Queen Elizabeth II is the monarch of the United Kingdom.

(3) The parks were originally used as recreation for the royal family, but have been opened to the general public over the last two centuries. The largest of the Royal Parks in Central London are The Regent's Park, Hyde Park, St. James's Park, Green Park, and Kensington Gardens, although the largest Royal Park in London is Richmond Park.

(4) Regent's Park is very big, and there are many attractions and things to do for both London citizens and travelers. Immediately, I was amazed with the beautiful scenery and the plethora of trees and ponds. It is also a very popular site for physical activities and exercise. There are several fields that are known as "sport pitches" that are used for soccer, cricket, rugby, and other sports. The park is lined with pedestrian trails, and there were many walkers and joggers.

(5) Regent's Park was my favorite park because it housed the London Zoo. In an attempt to create a close replica to the animals' natural environment, the animals were in the open, out of cages, in enclosed areas. My favorite attraction was the Galapagos Tortoises exhibit, as they were the largest tortoises I had ever seen.

(6) We all had a great time in London, and I loved seeing all of the great London attractions. It surprised me that with everything available to do in London, my favorite part of the city was a Royal Park.

24. What is the purpose for paragraph 1?
    a. To talk about the narrator's parents' anniversary
    b. To introduce why the family was in London
    c. To explain what it was like to travel to London
    d. To explain why the narrator liked central London

25. What does the word replica mean in paragraph 5?
    a. Item
    b. Family
    c. Copy
    d. Habitat

26. What is the largest Royal Park in London?
    a. The Regent's Park
    b. Hyde Park
    c. Kensington Gardens
    d. Richmond Park

27. Where is Regent's Park located?
    a. Westminster Abbey
    b. City of Westminster
    c. South London
    d. City of London

28. What does the word plethora mean paragraph 4?
    a. Excess
    b. Ugliness
    c. Few
    d. Color

29. What reason did the narrator state for Regent's Park being her favorite?
    a. It was the prettiest park
    b. It was close to Hyde Park
    c. It housed the London Zoo
    d. It had fields for cricket

30. What was the original use for the Royal Parks?
    a. To house Royal Zoos
    b. It was where the monarch ruled
    c. It was the site of the monarch's garden
    d. Recreation for the royal family

31. What are "sport pitches"?
    a. Pitchers for sport teams
    b. Sport fields
    c. Attractions in the zoo
    d. Pedestrian trails

32. How many Royal Parks are in Greater London?
    a. One
    b. Seventeen
    c. Eight
    d. Five

33. What was the narrator's favorite attraction at the zoo?
   a. Galapagos Tortoises
   b. The atrium
   c. Butterfly Paradise
   d. Reptile House

34. Why are some parks known as "Royal Parks"?
   a. Queen Elizabeth II likes them
   b. The parks are land originally owned by the monarchy
   c. The parks are the biggest parks in London
   d. It is where the head of state lives

35. Why was it surprising to the narrator that a park was her favorite part of the city?
   a. Because parks are normally really boring
   b. Because there is normally not a zoo at a park
   c. Because the park is ugly
   d. Because there are so many other fun attractions in London

36. What is the general purpose of this essay?
   a. To talk about Regent's Park
   b. To talk about Queen Elizabeth II
   c. To talk about the narrator's trip to London
   d. To talk about the London Zoo

Questions 37 –46 pertain to the following passage:

The Little Big Surprise

(1) This cannot be happening to me, I thought. Not at my age. Not at their age! This was without a doubt, the worst possible thing that could be happening to me, and it was going to change all of our lives forever.
(2) It was a Sunday morning in late February. I had been studying all morning for a vocabulary test I had later in the week. I thought it was going to be my biggest problem for the week. I had no idea what was coming my way. My mom knocked on my door and asked me to come downstairs. We were going to be having a family meeting.
(3) Family meeting? I thought. It seemed really strange. We never had family meetings. Nothing was ever so formal. It had been just my mom, my dad, and me for twelve years, and whenever there was anything to be discussed, they just told me. But a family meeting? This was weird.
(4) I looked at my last flashcard and went downstairs. My parents were both sitting at the table and had very serious looks on their faces. At first, I thought I must have been in trouble, but I hadn't done anything wrong, at least that I knew. Then I saw a small smile come over my mom's face. She was really happy.
(5) I sat down. "What's going on?" I asked. "Is something wrong?"
(6) And then my mom said the most awful thing I could ever imagine.
(7) "You are going to have a new brother or sister!"
(8) I could not even process the information. Nothing made sense. They could not be having another baby! I was old! They were even older! I was in

- 43 -

junior high, and I would be going to high school soon. People in high school didn't have baby brothers or sisters, did they? I was an only child! I was supposed to always be the only child!

(9) I immediately left the table and stormed into my bedroom. I went back to my flashcards and tried to forget everything that they had just said. I didn't want to think about things changing. I liked my life. I did not want everything to be changed and ruined.

(10) Over the next few months, I watched as my mother's stomach grew. It was amazing how quickly it all happened. Once it started, it seemed to grow more each week. My dad would laugh and say that the baby must be pretty big. It was interesting to think about a baby growing, but I did not want to think about anything.

(11) During the summer, my parents turned their office into a nursery. They painted the room a pale yellow color and bought a crib. Soon the room was filled with diapers, wipes, and baby powder. Everything smelled weird, like a baby.

(12) I tried not to think about how the house was looking different and that my mom was getting bigger every day. But then in the beginning of August, right before I was supposed to start school again, my mom said she had to go to the hospital. And my heart sank.

(13) "Is there something wrong?" I asked. "Are you okay? Is the baby okay?"

(14) My mom smiled at me. I thought that was pretty weird since she said she needed to be at the hospital.

(15) "The baby is fine," she said. "The baby is just ready to be born."

(16) My dad grabbed her overnight bad, and we raced to the car.

(17) A few hours later, my dad came out to see my grandparents and me in the waiting room. He had a big smile on his face and called out to me.

(18) "Do you want to meet your brother?" he said.

(19) A brother? I have a brother? I couldn't believe it. I walked into the room and saw my mom holding a baby. The nurses said he was a big baby, but he looked so little sitting in my mom's arms.

(20) "That's my brother," I said, and I could feel a huge smile spreading across my face. "I have a brother." It was amazing. I had someone to share my life and whom I could teach about the world.

(21) "His name is Gavin," my mom said. "Do you want to hold him?"

(22) I took my brother in my arms and smiled.

(23) "You're late," I said to him. "You should have been here years ago, but I'm glad you are here now."

37. What mood is created in paragraph 1?
    a. Sadness
    b. Anger
    c. Suspense
    d. Fear

38. Why did the narrator think the family meeting was weird?
    a. Family meetings were usually on Saturdays
    b. They had never had a family meeting before
    c. They only had family meetings when the narrator was in trouble
    d. Family meetings would not normally take place while the narrator was studying

39. What did the narrator think his biggest problem of the week was going to be?
    a. A vocabulary test
    b. A math test
    c. A sports competition
    d. The cold weather in February

40. What is the central conflict?
    a. The narrator does not like babies
    b. The narrator thinks his parents won't love him anymore
    c. The narrator is afraid something is wrong with the baby
    d. The narrator does not want his life to change

41. What does the word process mean in paragraph 8?
    a. Handle
    b. Understand
    c. Maintain
    d. Enjoy

42. What was a main reason the narrator used for why his parents could not have another baby?
    a. His parents were old
    b. They did not have room in the house
    c. There would be more family meetings
    d. The baby would get in too much trouble

43. In paragraph 10, the phrase "I did not want to think about anything" helps the reader to understand:
    a. The narrator does not like to think
    b. The narrator is confused
    c. The narrator thinks a baby growing is weird
    d. The narrator does not want his life to change

44. Why did the narrator's heart sink when his mom had to go to the hospital?
    a. He knew the baby was coming
    b. He was not ready yet
    c. He was afraid there was something wrong with his mom or the baby
    d. His dad was not home.

45. How is the narrator's internal conflict resolved?
    a. He does well on the vocabulary test
    b. His brother is born and he realizes he loves him
    c. He thinks his life won't change that much
    d. He started a new school year

46. Why did the narrator tell his brother he was late?
    a. He wished he had born earlier in his life
    b. He wished his brother had born earlier in the day
    c. It took a long time to be born
    d. His due date was earlier

Questions 47 – 50 pertain to the following passage:

What's Real About It?

(1) I suppose I don't understand why it is called reality television. It has been argued that reality television has been a part of television since the beginnings of television programming. Through game shows and daytime talk shows, real people, as in non-actors, have made appearances on television for the entertainment of others. A new genre of reality television that became the new phenomenon, however, was introduced in the year 2000, with shows such as "Survivor."

(2) The idea behind "Survivor" is like many in reality television. There are contestants, they are put in extreme situations, and in the end, someone wins a prize. The other main style of reality television involves cameras following someone around as they live their daily life.

(3) My confusion comes from the title of reality. Reality means the state of which things actually exist, but reality television does not display the state in which life actually exists. In real life, not many people will be deserted on a distant island or forced to live in a house with several strangers. Additionally, cameras do not follow people around on a normal day. People live their lives, and exist in a reality that is not meant for entertainment or for masses of people to watch.

(4) It is no surprise to discover that most audiences find it interesting to watch people who are not actors on television. There is something intriguing about fame for the average person. It is as if the viewer can relate more to the show that he or she is watching, because it is real people put in fake situations rather than fake people and characters acting in life-like situations. However, there cannot be anything called reality television that would be both an accurate description of life and provide necessary entertainment.

47. What is the main argument of this essay?
    a. Reality television is not entertainment
    b. Reality television uses actors
    c. The basis of reality television is not reality
    d. Most people do not enjoy reality television

48. Which of the following statements is not an opinion?
    a. "Reality means the state of which things actually exist"
    b. "There is something intriguing about fame for the average person"
    c. "I suppose I don't understand why it is called reality television"
    d. "It is as if the viewer can relate more to the show that he or she is watching"

49. How long does the author say that reality television has been a part of television?
    a. Since 2000
    b. Since the early 1950s
    c. Within the last ten years
    d. Since the beginning of television programming

50. Why does the author assume audiences like to watch reality television?
    a. They enjoy watching real-life situations
    b. Viewers can relate more to real people than actors
    c. They wish they could be celebrities
    d. They want to win prizes

Answers and Explanations

TEKS Standard §110.19(b)(8)
1. C: The author provides several images in paragraph 1, such as the day being cloudless, the sun beating down, skin burning, and sweating that create the image of that it is hot outside.

TEKS Standard §110.19(b)(8)
2. D: In paragraph 1, the author creates several images to display the overwhelming heat outside. Johnny fanning his face with his glove is another example.

TEKS Standard §110.19(b)(6)
3. A: Paragraph 16 explains that Max planned to spend the entire summer training for baseball. In paragraph 20, Max's mom explains that there is more to life than baseball and that she wants him to spend his summer having fun with his friends.

TEKS Standard §110.19(b)(6)(C)
4. B: The story is told from Max's point of view, in the first person. The point of view is also limited because the audience does not receive any other character's thoughts and feelings.

TEKS Standard §110.19(b)(6)
5. C: It is explained in paragraph 1 that Max is sitting on the bench and is not playing in the game. In paragraph 5, Max explains that when he saw the coach pointing at him, he knew he was not imagining things.

TEKS Standard §110.19(b)(8)
6. A: Max and the pitcher are both in pressure situations. Max wants to hit the ball and help his team, and the pitcher wants to help his own team by not letting Max hit the ball. The mood is tense, as the author creates tension.

TEKS Standard §110.19(b)(6)
7. B: In paragraph 9, Max explains that he swung as hard as he could. In paragraph 10, Max says, "I didn't feel anything," and in paragraph 11, it is explained that Max struck out. He was confused because he did not hit the ball. He swung and he missed.

TEKS Standard §110.19(b)(8)
8. D: In paragraph 16, it is explained that Max felt like he had let everyone down and disappointed all of his teammates after he struck out and the team lost. In paragraph 17, Max says that he decided to spend the entire summer training for baseball.

TEKS Standard §110.19(b)(2)(A) and (2)(B)
9. C: Install means to put in.

TEKS Standard §110.19(b)(2)(A) and (2)(B)
10. B: Stern means severe or harsh.

TEKS Standard §110.19(b)(6)(B)
11. A: Max struggles throughout the essay to see that it was not anyone's fault that the team lost the baseball game. In believing that he let his team down, Max wants to practice

baseball all summer and get better, but he is no longer having fun. His conflict is in having fun with baseball.

TEKS Standard §110.19(b)(6)(B)
12. D: In paragraph 23, it is explained that Max smiled and was having fun when it was his turn to bat, and he ended up hitting a homerun.

TEKS Standard §110.19(b)(10)(B)
13. C: To say, "everything about the theater was great," cannot be proven as fact. This is strictly an opinion that could differ with another person.

TEKS Standard §110.19(b)(2)(A) and (2)(B)
14. A: Inception means the starting point or establishment of something.

TEKS Standard §110.19(b)(7) and (10)
15. D: Paragraph 1 states, "The Alamo Drafthouse Cinema is like no other movie theater experience. For one thing, no one under the age of eighteen is allowed into the theater without a parent or guardian, no matter the rating of the film."

TEKS Standard §110.19(b)(7) and (10)
16. C: Paragraph 2 states, "The Alamo Drafthouse Cinema originated in Austin, Texas."

TEKS Standard §110.19(b)(2)(A) and (2)(B)
17. B: Intricate means extremely complicated or detailed.

TEKS Standard §110.19(b)(7) and (10)
18. A: In paragraph 3, the narrator states that the decorations in the lobby were "three-dimensional, and made me feel like I was a part of the theater, or maybe a part of the movie."

TEKS Standard §110.19(b)(10)
19. D: In paragraph 4, the narrator explains that, "Everything about the theater was great."

TEKS Standard §110.19(b)(7) and (10)
20. C: Paragraph 4 states, "Throughout the movie, he walked as quickly as he could so that he would not disrupt the movie."

TEKS Standard §110.19(b)(7) and (10)
21. D: Paragraph 3 states, "I was surprised to see that it looked like a normal movie theater expect for a large tabletop that extended across the length of every aisle of seats."

TEKS Standard §110.19(b)(7) and (10)
22. B: The essay begins with an introduction as to why the narrator was at the theater, followed by a brief history of the theater to provide the reader with context, and ending with the narrator's own personal experience at the theater.

TEKS Standard §110.19(b)(7) and (10)
23. A: Austin, Houston, San Antonio, and Winchester all have at least one Alamo Drafthouse Cinema location.

TEKS Standard §110.19(b)(7) and (10)

24. B: The essay describes The Regent's Park in London, and the purpose of paragraph 1 is to introduce the essay and explain why the narrator was in London and discovered The Regent's Park.

TEKS Standard §110.19(b)(2)(A) and (2)(B)

25. C: Replica means an exact copy of something, especially on a smaller scale.

TEKS Standard §110.19(b)(7) and (10)

26. D: Paragraph 3 states that "the largest Royal Park in London is Richmond Park."

TEKS Standard §110.19(b)(7) and (10)

27. B: In paragraph 1, it is explained that Regent's Park is located in "the City of Westminster in central London."

TEKS Standard §10.19(b)(2)(A) and (2)(B)

28. A: Plethora means an excess of something.

TEKS Standard §110.19(b)(7) and (10)

29. C: Paragraph 5 states, "Regent's Park was my favorite park because it housed the London Zoo."

TEKS Standard §110.19(b)(7) and (10)

30. D: Paragraph 3 states, "The parks were originally used as recreation for the royal family."

TEKS Standard §110.19(b)(7) and (10)

31. B: Paragraph 4 states, "There are several fields that are known as 'sport pitches' that are used for soccer, cricket, rugby, and other sports."

TEKS Standard §110.19(b)(7) and (10)

32. C: Paragraph 2 states, "The Regent's Park, which most people refer to as "Regent's Park," is one of the eight Royal Parks in Greater London."

TEKS Standard §110.19(b)(7) and (10)

33. A: In paragraph 5, the narrator states, "My favorite attraction was the Galapagos Tortoises exhibit."

TEKS Standard §110.19(b)(7) and (10)

34. B: Paragraph 2 states, "A Royal Park is land that was once owned by the royal monarchy, or crown, of the United Kingdom."

TEKS Standard §110.19(b)(7) and (10)

35. D: In paragraph 6, the narrator states, "It surprised me that with everything available to do in London, my favorite part of the city was a Royal Park."

TEKS Standard §110.19(b)(7) and (10)

36. A: The majority of the essay is focused on The Regent's Park in central London. The attractions are discussed, as well as the history and purpose of the park.

TEKS Standard §110.19(b)(8)

37. C: The author creates a mood of suspense by not explaining what has happened to make the narrator feel like something was "the worst possible thing that could be happening to me."

TEKS Standard §110.19(b)(6)

38. B: Paragraph 3 states, "We never had family meetings." The narrator thinks that the meeting is strange because they had never had meetings before.

TEKS Standard §110.19(b)(6)

39. A: In paragraph 2, the narrator explains that he was studying for a vocabulary test he had later in the week. He then mentions that he thought it was going to be the biggest problem of the week.

TEKS Standard §110.19(b)(6)(B)

40. D: Throughout the essay, the narrator explains that he likes his life and does not want things to change. He expresses that he is the only child and was supposed to always be an only child. In paragraph 9, he states, "I didn't want to think about things changing. I liked my life. I did not want everything to be changed and ruined."

TEKS Standard §110.19(b)(2)(A) and (2)(B)

41. B: When used as a verb, process means to gain acceptance or an understanding.

TEKS Standard §110.19(b)(6)

42. A: The narrator mentions in both paragraph 1 and paragraph 8 that he felt as though his parents were too old to have another baby and that he was too old to have a baby sibling.

TEKS Standard §110.19(b)(6)

43. D: The narrator mentions in paragraph 9, "I didn't want to think about things changing." In the next paragraph the narrator mentions that even though it was interesting to think about a baby growing, he still did not want to think about anything, meaning his life changing.

TEKS Standard §110.19(b)(6)

44. C: In paragraph 13, the narrator asks his mom if something is wrong and if she and the baby are okay.

TEKS Standard §110.19(b)(6)(B)

45. B: In paragraph 20, the narrator states, "It was amazing. I had someone to share my life and whom I could teach about the world." The narrator comes to an understanding that even though his life is going to change, it is okay because he loves his brother and his new life will be good with his brother.

TEKS Standard §110.19(b)(6)

46. A: In paragraph 23, the narrator says, "'You should have been here years ago, but I'm glad you are here now.'" The narrator states that he wishes his brother had around sooner, but he is glad to have him now.

TEKS Standard §110.19(b)(11)

47. C: The author states in paragraph 3, "reality television does not display the state of which life actually exists." Throughout the essay, the narrator discusses the ways in which reality television does not reflect reality.

TEKS Standard §110.19(b)(10)(B)

48. A: In this statement, the author is providing a factual definition of a word.

TEKS Standard §110.19(b)(11)

49. D: Paragraph 1 states, "It has been argued that reality television has been a part of television since the beginnings of television programming."

TEKS Standard §110.19(b)(11) and (10)(B)

50. B: In paragraph 4, the author explains her assumptions that viewers relate more to real people than actors. "It is as if the viewer can relate more to the show that he or she is watching, because it is real people put in fake situations rather than fake people and characters acting in life-like situations."

Success Strategies

The most important thing you can do is to ignore your fears and jump into the test immediately- do not be overwhelmed by any strange-sounding terms. You have to jump into the test like jumping into a pool- all at once is the easiest way.

Make Predictions

As you read and understand the question, try to guess what the answer will be. Remember that several of the answer choices are wrong, and once you begin reading them, your mind will immediately become cluttered with answer choices designed to throw you off. Your mind is typically the most focused immediately after you have read the question and digested its contents. If you can, try to predict what the correct answer will be. You may be surprised at what you can predict.

Quickly scan the choices and see if your prediction is in the listed answer choices. If it is, then you can be quite confident that you have the right answer. It still won't hurt to check the other answer choices, but most of the time, you've got it!

Answer the Question

It may seem obvious to only pick answer choices that answer the question, but the test writers can create some excellent answer choices that are wrong. Don't pick an answer just because it sounds right, or you believe it to be true. It MUST answer the question. Once you've made your selection, always go back and check it against the question and make sure that you didn't misread the question, and the answer choice does answer the question posed.

Benchmark

After you read the first answer choice, decide if you think it sounds correct or not. If it doesn't, move on to the next answer choice. If it does, mentally mark that answer choice. This doesn't mean that you've definitely selected it as your answer choice, it just means that it's the best you've seen thus far. Go ahead and read the next choice. If the next choice is worse than the one you've already selected, keep going to the next answer choice. If the next choice is better than the choice you've already selected, mentally mark the new answer choice as your best guess.

The first answer choice that you select becomes your standard. Every other answer choice must be benchmarked against that standard. That choice is correct until proven otherwise by another answer choice beating it out. Once you've decided that no other answer choice seems as good, do one final check to ensure that your answer choice answers the question posed.

Valid Information

Don't discount any of the information provided in the question. Every piece of information may be necessary to determine the correct answer. None of the information in the question is there to throw you off (while the answer choices will certainly have information to throw you off). If two seemingly unrelated topics are discussed, don't ignore either. You can be confident there is a relationship, or it wouldn't be included in the question, and you are probably going to have to determine what is that relationship to find the answer.

Avoid "Fact Traps"

Don't get distracted by a choice that is factually true. Your search is for the answer that answers the question. Stay focused and don't fall for an answer that is true but incorrect. Always go back to the question and make sure you're choosing an answer that actually answers the question and is not just a true statement. An answer can be factually correct, but it MUST answer the question asked. Additionally, two answers can both be seemingly correct, so be sure to read all of the answer choices, and make sure that you get the one that BEST answers the question.

Milk the Question

Some of the questions may throw you completely off. They might deal with a subject you have not been exposed to, or one that you haven't reviewed in years. While your lack of knowledge about the subject will be a hindrance, the question itself can give you many clues that will help you find the correct answer. Read the question carefully and look for clues. Watch particularly for adjectives and nouns describing difficult terms or words that you don't recognize. Regardless of if you completely understand a word or not, replacing it with a synonym either provided or one you more familiar with may help you to understand what the questions are asking. Rather than wracking your mind about specific detailed information concerning a difficult term or word, try to use mental substitutes that are easier to understand.

The Trap of Familiarity

Don't just choose a word because you recognize it. On difficult questions, you may not recognize a number of words in the answer choices. The test writers don't put "make-believe" words on the test; so don't think that just because you only recognize all the words in one answer choice means that answer choice must be correct. If you only recognize words in one answer choice, then focus on that one. Is it correct? Try your best to determine if it is correct. If it is, that is great, but if it doesn't, eliminate it. Each word and answer choice you eliminate increases your chances of getting the question correct, even if you then have to guess among the unfamiliar choices.

Eliminate Answers

Eliminate choices as soon as you realize they are wrong. But be careful! Make sure you consider all of the possible answer choices. Just because one appears right, doesn't mean that the next one won't be even better! The test writers will usually put more than one good answer choice for every question, so read all of them. Don't worry if you are stuck between two that seem right. By getting down to just two remaining possible choices, your odds are now 50/50. Rather than wasting too much time, play the odds. You are guessing, but guessing wisely, because you've been able to knock out some of the answer choices that you know are wrong. If you are eliminating choices and realize that the last answer choice you are left with is also obviously wrong, don't panic. Start over and consider each choice again. There may easily be something that you missed the first time and will realize on the second pass.

Tough Questions

If you are stumped on a problem or it appears too hard or too difficult, don't waste time. Move on! Remember though, if you can quickly check for obviously incorrect answer choices, your chances of guessing correctly are greatly improved. Before you completely give up, at least try to knock out a couple of possible answers. Eliminate what you can and then guess at the remaining answer choices before moving on.

Brainstorm

If you get stuck on a difficult question, spend a few seconds quickly brainstorming. Run through the complete list of possible answer choices. Look at each choice and ask yourself, "Could this answer the question satisfactorily?" Go through each answer choice and consider it independently of the other. By systematically going through all possibilities, you may find something that you would otherwise overlook. Remember that when you get stuck, it's important to try to keep moving.

Read Carefully

Understand the problem. Read the question and answer choices carefully. Don't miss the question because you misread the terms. You have plenty of time to read each question thoroughly and make sure you understand what is being asked. Yet a happy medium must be attained, so don't waste too much time. You must read carefully, but efficiently.

Face Value

When in doubt, use common sense. Always accept the situation in the problem at face value. Don't read too much into it. These problems will not require you to make huge leaps of logic. The test writers aren't trying to throw you off with a cheap trick. If you have to go beyond creativity and make a leap of logic in order to have an answer choice answer the question, then you should look at the other answer choices. Don't overcomplicate the problem by creating theoretical relationships or explanations that will warp time or space. These are normal problems rooted in reality. It's just that the applicable relationship or explanation may not be readily apparent and you have to figure things out. Use your common sense to interpret anything that isn't clear.

Prefixes

If you're having trouble with a word in the question or answer choices, try dissecting it. Take advantage of every clue that the word might include. Prefixes and suffixes can be a huge help. Usually they allow you to determine a basic meaning. Pre- means before, post-means after, pro - is positive, de- is negative. From these prefixes and suffixes, you can get an idea of the general meaning of the word and try to put it into context. Beware though of any traps. Just because con is the opposite of pro, doesn't necessarily mean congress is the opposite of progress!

Hedge Phrases

Watch out for critical "hedge" phrases, such as likely, may, can, will often, sometimes, often, almost, mostly, usually, generally, rarely, sometimes. Question writers insert these hedge phrases to cover every possibility. Often an answer choice will be wrong simply because it leaves no room for exception. Avoid answer choices that have definitive words like "exactly," and "always".

Switchback Words

Stay alert for "switchbacks". These are the words and phrases frequently used to alert you to shifts in thought. The most common switchback word is "but". Others include although, however, nevertheless, on the other hand, even though, while, in spite of, despite, regardless of.

- 55 -

New Information

Correct answer choices will rarely have completely new information included. Answer choices typically are straightforward reflections of the material asked about and will directly relate to the question. If a new piece of information is included in an answer choice that doesn't even seem to relate to the topic being asked about, then that answer choice is likely incorrect. All of the information needed to answer the question is usually provided for you, and so you should not have to make guesses that are unsupported or choose answer choices that require unknown information that cannot be reasoned on its own.

Time Management

On technical questions, don't get lost on the technical terms. Don't spend too much time on any one question. If you don't know what a term means, then since you don't have a dictionary, odds are you aren't going to get much further. You should immediately recognize terms as whether or not you know them. If you don't, work with the other clues that you have, the other answer choices and terms provided, but don't waste too much time trying to figure out a difficult term.

Contextual Clues

Look for contextual clues. An answer can be right but not correct. The contextual clues will help you find the answer that is most right and is correct. Understand the context in which a phrase or statement is made. This will help you make important distinctions.

Don't Panic

Panicking will not answer any questions for you. Therefore, it isn't helpful. When you first see the question, if your mind goes blank, take a deep breath. Force yourself to mechanically go through the steps of solving the problem and using the strategies you've learned.

Pace Yourself

Don't get clock fever. It's easy to be overwhelmed when you're looking at a page full of questions, your mind is full of random thoughts and feeling confused, and the clock is ticking down faster than you would like. Calm down and maintain the pace that you have set for yourself. As long as you are on track by monitoring your pace, you are guaranteed to have enough time for yourself. When you get to the last few minutes of the test, it may seem like you won't have enough time left, but if you only have as many questions as you should have left at that point, then you're right on track!

Answer Selection

The best way to pick an answer choice is to eliminate all of those that are wrong, until only one is left and confirm that is the correct answer. Sometimes though, an answer choice may immediately look right. Be careful! Take a second to make sure that the other choices are not equally obvious. Don't make a hasty mistake. There are only two times that you should stop before checking other answers. First is when you are positive that the answer choice you have selected is correct. Second is when time is almost out and you have to make a quick guess!

Check Your Work

Since you will probably not know every term listed and the answer to every question, it is important that you get credit for the ones that you do know. Don't miss any questions through careless mistakes. If at all possible, try to take a second to look back over your answer selection and make sure you've selected the correct answer choice and haven't made a costly careless mistake (such as marking an answer choice that you didn't mean to mark). This quick double check should more than pay for itself in caught mistakes for the time it costs.

Beware of Directly Quoted Answers

Sometimes an answer choice will repeat word for word a portion of the question or reference section. However, beware of such exact duplication – it may be a trap! More than likely, the correct choice will paraphrase or summarize a point, rather than being exactly the same wording.

Slang

Scientific sounding answers are better than slang ones. An answer choice that begins "To compare the outcomes..." is much more likely to be correct than one that begins "Because some people insisted..."

Extreme Statements

Avoid wild answers that throw out highly controversial ideas that are proclaimed as established fact. An answer choice that states the "process should be used in certain situations, if..." is much more likely to be correct than one that states the "process should be discontinued completely." The first is a calm rational statement and doesn't even make a definitive, uncompromising stance, using a hedge word "if" to provide wiggle room, whereas the second choice is a radical idea and far more extreme.

Answer Choice Families

When you have two or more answer choices that are direct opposites or parallels, one of them is usually the correct answer. For instance, if one answer choice states "x increases" and another answer choice states "x decreases" or "y increases," then those two or three answer choices are very similar in construction and fall into the same family of answer choices. A family of answer choices is when two or three answer choices are very similar in construction, and yet often have a directly opposite meaning. Usually the correct answer choice will be in that family of answer choices. The "odd man out" or answer choice that doesn't seem to fit the parallel construction of the other answer choices is more likely to be incorrect.

How to Overcome Test Anxiety

The very nature of tests caters to some level of anxiety, nervousness or tension, just as we feel for any important event that occurs in our lives. A little bit of anxiety or nervousness can be a good thing. It helps us with motivation, and makes achievement just that much sweeter. However, too much anxiety can be a problem; especially if it hinders our ability to function and perform.

"Test anxiety," is the term that refers to the emotional reactions that some test-takers experience when faced with a test or exam. Having a fear of testing and exams is based upon a rational fear, since the test-taker's performance can shape the course of an academic career. Nevertheless, experiencing excessive fear of examinations will only interfere with the test-takers ability to perform, and his/her chances to be successful.

There are a large variety of causes that can contribute to the development and sensation of test anxiety. These include, but are not limited to lack of performance and worrying about issues surrounding the test.

Lack of Preparation

Lack of preparation can be identified by the following behaviors or situations:

Not scheduling enough time to study, and therefore cramming the night before the test or exam
Managing time poorly, to create the sensation that there is not enough time to do everything
Failing to organize the text information in advance, so that the study material consists of the entire text and not simply the pertinent information
Poor overall studying habits

Worrying, on the other hand, can be related to both the test taker, or many other factors around him/her that will be affected by the results of the test. These include worrying about:

Previous performances on similar exams, or exams in general
How friends and other students are achieving
The negative consequences that will result from a poor grade or failure

There are three primary elements to test anxiety. Physical components, which involve the same typical bodily reactions as those to acute anxiety (to be discussed below). Emotional factors have to do with fear or panic. Mental or cognitive issues concerning attention spans and memory abilities.

Physical Signals

There are many different symptoms of test anxiety, and these are not limited to mental and emotional strain. Frequently there are a range of physical signals that will let a test taker know that he/she is suffering from test anxiety. These bodily changes can include the following:

Perspiring
Sweaty palms
Wet, trembling hands
Nausea
Dry mouth
A knot in the stomach
Headache
Faintness
Muscle tension
Aching shoulders, back and neck
Rapid heart beat
Feeling too hot/cold

To recognize the sensation of test anxiety, a test-taker should monitor him/herself for the following sensations:

The physical distress symptoms as listed above
Emotional sensitivity, expressing emotional feelings such as the need to cry or laugh too much, or a sensation of anger or helplessness
A decreased ability to think, causing the test-taker to blank out or have racing thoughts that are hard to organize or control.

Though most students will feel some level of anxiety when faced with a test or exam, the majority can cope with that anxiety and maintain it at a manageable level. However, those who cannot are faced with a very real and very serious condition, which can and should be controlled for the immeasurable benefit of this sufferer.

Naturally, these sensations lead to negative results for the testing experience. The most common effects of test anxiety have to do with nervousness and mental blocking.

Nervousness

Nervousness can appear in several different levels:

The test-taker's difficulty, or even inability to read and understand the questions on the test
The difficulty or inability to organize thoughts to a coherent form
The difficulty or inability to recall key words and concepts relating to the testing questions (especially essays)
The receipt of poor grades on a test, though the test material was well known by the test taker

Conversely, a person may also experience mental blocking, which involves:

Blanking out on test questions
Only remembering the correct answers to the questions when the test has already finished.

Fortunately for test anxiety sufferers, beating these feelings, to a large degree, has to do with proper preparation. When a test taker has a feeling of preparedness, then anxiety will be dramatically lessened.

The first step to resolving anxiety issues is to distinguish which of the two types of anxiety are being suffered. If the anxiety is a direct result of a lack of preparation, this should be considered a normal reaction, and the anxiety level (as opposed to the test results) shouldn't be anything to worry about. However, if, when adequately prepared, the test-taker still panics, blanks out, or seems to overreact, this is not a fully rational reaction. While this can be considered normal too, there are many ways to combat and overcome these effects.

Remember that anxiety cannot be entirely eliminated, however, there are ways to minimize it, to make the anxiety easier to manage. Preparation is one of the best ways to minimize test anxiety. Therefore the following techniques are wise in order to best fight off any anxiety that may want to build.

To begin with, try to avoid cramming before a test, whenever it is possible. By trying to memorize an entire term's worth of information in one day, you'll be shocking your system, and not giving yourself a very good chance to absorb the information. This is an easy path to anxiety, so for those who suffer from test anxiety, cramming should not even be considered an option.

Instead of cramming, work throughout the semester to combine all of the material which is presented throughout the semester, and work on it gradually as the course goes by, making sure to master the main concepts first, leaving minor details for a week or so before the test.

To study for the upcoming exam, be sure to pose questions that may be on the examination, to gauge the ability to answer them by integrating the ideas from your texts, notes and lectures, as well as any supplementary readings.

If it is truly impossible to cover all of the information that was covered in that particular term, concentrate on the most important portions, that can be covered very well. Learn these concepts as best as possible, so that when the test comes, a goal can be made to use these concepts as presentations of your knowledge.

In addition to study habits, changes in attitude are critical to beating a struggle with test anxiety. In fact, an improvement of the perspective over the entire test-taking experience can actually help a test taker to enjoy studying and therefore improve the overall experience. Be certain not to overemphasize the significance of the grade - know that the result of the test is neither a reflection of self worth, nor is it a measure of intelligence; one grade will not predict a person's future success.

To improve an overall testing outlook, the following steps should be tried:

Keeping in mind that the most reasonable expectation for taking a test is to expect to try to demonstrate as much of what you know as you possibly can.
Reminding ourselves that a test is only one test; this is not the only one, and there will be others.
The thought of thinking of oneself in an irrational, all-or-nothing term should be avoided at all costs.
A reward should be designated for after the test, so there's something to look forward to. Whether it be going to a movie, going out to eat, or simply visiting friends, schedule it in advance, and do it no matter what result is expected on the exam.

Test-takers should also keep in mind that the basics are some of the most important things, even beyond anti-anxiety techniques and studying. Never neglect the basic social, emotional and biological needs, in order to try to absorb information. In order to best achieve, these three factors must be held as just as important as the studying itself.

Study Steps

Remember the following important steps for studying:

Maintain healthy nutrition and exercise habits. Continue both your recreational activities and social pass times. These both contribute to your physical and emotional well being.
Be certain to get a good amount of sleep, especially the night before the test, because when you're overtired you are not able to perform to the best of your best ability.
Keep the studying pace to a moderate level by taking breaks when they are needed, and varying the work whenever possible, to keep the mind fresh instead of getting bored. When enough studying has been done that all the material that can be learned has been learned, and the test taker is prepared for the test, stop studying and do something relaxing such as listening to music, watching a movie, or taking a warm bubble bath.

There are also many other techniques to minimize the uneasiness or apprehension that is experienced along with test anxiety before, during, or even after the examination. In fact, there are a great deal of things that can be done to stop anxiety from interfering with lifestyle and performance. Again, remember that anxiety will not be eliminated entirely, and it shouldn't be. Otherwise that "up" feeling for exams would not exist, and most of us depend on that sensation to perform better than usual. However, this anxiety has to be at a level that is manageable.

Of course, as we have just discussed, being prepared for the exam is half the battle right away. Attending all classes, finding out what knowledge will be expected on the exam, and knowing the exam schedules are easy steps to lowering anxiety. Keeping up with work will remove the need to cram, and efficient study habits will eliminate wasted time. Studying should be done in an ideal location for concentration, so that it is simple to become interested in the material and give it complete attention. A method such as SQ3R (Survey, Question, Read, Recite, Review) is a wonderful key to follow to make sure that the study habits are as effective as possible, especially in the case of learning from a textbook. Flashcards are great techniques for memorization. Learning to take good notes will mean that notes will be full of useful information, so that less sifting will need to be done to seek out what is pertinent for studying. Reviewing notes after class and then again on occasion will keep the information fresh in the mind. From notes that have been taken summary sheets and outlines can be made for simpler reviewing.

A study group can also be a very motivational and helpful place to study, as there will be a sharing of ideas, all of the minds can work together, to make sure that everyone understands, and the studying will be made more interesting because it will be a social occasion.

Basically, though, as long as the test-taker remains organized and self confident, with efficient study habits, less time will need to be spent studying, and higher grades will be achieved.

To become self confident, there are many useful steps. The first of these is "self talk." It has been shown through extensive research, that self-talk for students who suffer from test anxiety, should be well monitored, in order to make sure that it contributes to self confidence as opposed to sinking the student. Frequently the self talk of test-anxious students is negative or self-defeating, thinking that everyone else is smarter and faster, that they always mess up, and that if they don't do well, they'll fail the entire course. It is important to decreasing anxiety that awareness is made of self talk. Try writing any negative self thoughts and then disputing them with a positive statement instead. Begin self-encouragement as though it was a friend speaking. Repeat positive statements to help reprogram the mind to believing in successes instead of failures.

Helpful Techniques

Other extremely helpful techniques include:

Self-visualization of doing well and reaching goals
While aiming for an "A" level of understanding, don't try to "overprotect" by setting your expectations lower. This will only convince the mind to stop studying in order to meet the lower expectations.
Don't make comparisons with the results or habits of other students. These are individual factors, and different things work for different people, causing different results.
Strive to become an expert in learning what works well, and what can be done in order to improve. Consider collecting this data in a journal.
Create rewards for after studying instead of doing things before studying that will only turn into avoidance behaviors.
Make a practice of relaxing - by using methods such as progressive relaxation, self-hypnosis, guided imagery, etc - in order to make relaxation an automatic sensation.
Work on creating a state of relaxed concentration so that concentrating will take on the focus of the mind, so that none will be wasted on worrying.
Take good care of the physical self by eating well and getting enough sleep.
Plan in time for exercise and stick to this plan.

Beyond these techniques, there are other methods to be used before, during and after the test that will help the test-taker perform well in addition to overcoming anxiety.

Before the exam comes the academic preparation. This involves establishing a study schedule and beginning at least one week before the actual date of the test. By doing this, the anxiety of not having enough time to study for the test will be automatically eliminated. Moreover, this will make the studying a much more effective experience, ensuring that the learning will be an easier process. This relieves much undue pressure on the test-taker.

Summary sheets, note cards, and flash cards with the main concepts and examples of these main concepts should be prepared in advance of the actual studying time. A topic should never be eliminated from this process. By omitting a topic because it isn't expected to be on the test is only setting up the test-taker for anxiety should it actually appear on the exam. Utilize the course syllabus for laying out the topics that should be studied. Carefully go over the notes that were made in class, paying special attention to any of the issues that the professor took special care to emphasize while lecturing in class. In the textbooks, use the chapter review, or if possible, the chapter tests, to begin your review.

It may even be possible to ask the instructor what information will be covered on the exam, or what the format of the exam will be (for example, multiple choice, essay, free form, true-false). Additionally, see if it is possible to find out how many questions will be on the test. If a review sheet or sample test has been offered by the professor, make good use of it, above anything else, for the preparation for the test. Another great resource for getting to know the examination is reviewing tests from previous semesters. Use these tests to review, and aim to achieve a 100% score on each of the possible topics. With a few exceptions, the goal that you set for yourself is the highest one that you will reach.

Take all of the questions that were assigned as homework, and rework them to any other possible course material. The more problems reworked, the more skill and confidence will form as a result. When forming the solution to a problem, write out each of the steps. Don't simply do head work. By doing as many steps on paper as possible, much clarification and therefore confidence will be formed. Do this with as many homework problems as possible, before checking the answers. By checking the answer after each problem, a reinforcement will exist, that will not be on the exam. Study situations should be as exam-like as possible, to prime the test-taker's system for the experience. By waiting to check the answers at the end, a psychological advantage will be formed, to decrease the stress factor.

Another fantastic reason for not cramming is the avoidance of confusion in concepts, especially when it comes to mathematics. 8-10 hours of study will become one hundred percent more effective if it is spread out over a week or at least several days, instead of doing it all in one sitting. Recognize that the human brain requires time in order to assimilate new material, so frequent breaks and a span of study time over several days will be much more beneficial.

Additionally, don't study right up until the point of the exam. Studying should stop a minimum of one hour before the exam begins. This allows the brain to rest and put things in their proper order. This will also provide the time to become as relaxed as possible when going into the examination room. The test-taker will also have time to eat well and eat sensibly. Know that the brain needs food as much as the rest of the

Copyright © Mometrix Media. You have been licensed one copy of this document for personal use only. Any other reproduction or redistribution is strictly prohibited. All rights reserved.

body. With enough food and enough sleep, as well as a relaxed attitude, the body and the mind are primed for success.

Avoid any anxious classmates who are talking about the exam. These students only spread anxiety, and are not worth sharing the anxious sentimentalities.

Before the test also involves creating a positive attitude, so mental preparation should also be a point of concentration. There are many keys to creating a positive attitude. Should fears become rushing in, make a visualization of taking the exam, doing well, and seeing an A written on the paper. Write out a list of affirmations that will bring a feeling of confidence, such as "I am doing well in my English class," "I studied well and know my material," "I enjoy this class." Even if the affirmations aren't believed at first, it sends a positive message to the subconscious which will result in an alteration of the overall belief system, which is the system that creates reality.

If a sensation of panic begins, work with the fear and imagine the very worst! Work through the entire scenario of not passing the test, failing the entire course, and dropping out of school, followed by not getting a job, and pushing a shopping cart through the dark alley where you'll live. This will place things into perspective! Then, practice deep breathing and create a visualization of the opposite situation - achieving an "A" on the exam, passing the entire course, receiving the degree at a graduation ceremony.

On the day of the test, there are many things to be done to ensure the best results, as well as the most calm outlook. The following stages are suggested in order to maximize test-taking potential:

Begin the examination day with a moderate breakfast, and avoid any coffee or beverages with caffeine if the test taker is prone to jitters. Even people who are used to managing caffeine can feel jittery or light-headed when it is taken on a test day.
Attempt to do something that is relaxing before the examination begins. As last minute cramming clouds the mastering of overall concepts, it is better to use this time to create a calming outlook.
Be certain to arrive at the test location well in advance, in order to provide time to select a location that is away from doors, windows and other distractions, as well as giving enough time to relax before the test begins.
Keep away from anxiety generating classmates who will upset the sensation of stability and relaxation that is being attempted before the exam.
Should the waiting period before the exam begins cause anxiety, create a self-distraction by reading a light magazine or something else that is relaxing and simple.

During the exam itself, read the entire exam from beginning to end, and find out how much time should be allotted to each individual problem. Once writing the exam, should more time be taken for a problem, it should be abandoned, in order to begin another problem. If there is time at the end, the unfinished problem can always be returned to and completed.

Read the instructions very carefully - twice - so that unpleasant surprises won't follow during or after the exam has ended.

When writing the exam, pretend that the situation is actually simply the completion of homework within a library, or at home. This will assist in forming a relaxed atmosphere, and will allow the brain extra focus for the complex thinking function.

Begin the exam with all of the questions with which the most confidence is felt. This will build the confidence level regarding the entire exam and will begin a quality momentum. This will also create encouragement for trying the problems where uncertainty resides.

Going with the "gut instinct" is always the way to go when solving a problem. Second guessing should be avoided at all costs. Have confidence in the ability to do well.

For essay questions, create an outline in advance that will keep the mind organized and make certain that all of the points are remembered. For multiple choice, read every answer, even if the correct one has been spotted - a better one may exist.

Continue at a pace that is reasonable and not rushed, in order to be able to work carefully. Provide enough time to go over the answers at the end, to check for small errors that can be corrected.

Should a feeling of panic begin, breathe deeply, and think of the feeling of the body releasing sand through its pores. Visualize a calm, peaceful place, and include all of the sights, sounds and sensations of this image. Continue the deep breathing, and take a few minutes to continue this with closed eyes. When all is well again, return to the test.

If a "blanking" occurs for a certain question, skip it and move on to the next question. There will be time to return to the other question later. Get everything done that can be done, first, to guarantee all the grades that can be compiled, and to build all of the confidence possible. Then return to the weaker questions to build the marks from there.

Remember, one's own reality can be created, so as long as the belief is there, success will follow. And remember: anxiety can happen later, right now, there's an exam to be written!

After the examination is complete, whether there is a feeling for a good grade or a bad grade, don't dwell on the exam, and be certain to follow through on the reward that was promised...and enjoy it! Don't dwell on any mistakes that have been made, as there is nothing that can be done at this point anyway.

Additionally, don't begin to study for the next test right away. Do something relaxing for a while, and let the mind relax and prepare itself to begin absorbing information again.

From the results of the exam - both the grade and the entire experience, be certain to learn from what has gone on. Perfect studying habits and work some more on confidence in order to make the next examination experience even better than the last one.

Learn to avoid places where openings occurred for laziness, procrastination and day dreaming.

Use the time between this exam and the next one to better learn to relax, even learning to relax on cue, so that any anxiety can be controlled during the next exam. Learn how to relax the body. Slouch in your chair if that helps. Tighten and then relax all of the different muscle groups, one group at a time, beginning with the feet and then working all the way up to the neck and face. This will ultimately relax the muscles more than they were to begin with. Learn how to breathe deeply and comfortably, and focus on this breathing going in and out as a relaxing thought. With every exhale, repeat the word "relax."

As common as test anxiety is, it is very possible to overcome it. Make yourself one of the test-takers who overcome this frustrating hindrance.

FREE Study Skills DVD Offer

Dear Customer,

Thank you for your purchase from Mometrix! We consider it an honor and privilege that you have purchased our product and want to ensure your satisfaction.

As a way of showing our appreciation and to help us better serve you, we have developed a Study Skills DVD that we would like to give you for <u>FREE</u>. **This DVD covers our "best practices" for studying for your exam, from using our study materials to preparing for the day of the test.**

All that we ask is that you email us your feedback that would describe your experience so far with our product. Good, bad or indifferent, we want to know what you think!

To get your **FREE Study Skills DVD**, email <u>freedvd@mometrix.com</u> with "FREE STUDY SKILLS DVD" in the subject line and the following information in the body of the email:

   a. The name of the product you purchased.

   b. Your product rating on a scale of 1-5, with 5 being the highest rating.

   c. Your feedback. It can be long, short, or anything in-between, just your impressions and experience so far with our product. Good feedback might include how our study material met your needs and will highlight features of the product that you found helpful.

   d. Your full name and shipping address where you would like us to send your free DVD.

If you have any questions or concerns, please don't hesitate to contact me directly.

Thanks again!

Sincerely,

Jay Willis
Vice President
<u>jay.willis@mometrix.com</u>
1-800-673-8175